"As a mother whose nest is soon to be empty, I appreciated the warmth and wisdom of Cheri's words. Today "mom" may be your job description, but before you know it, that will change and "Mom" will become a term of endearment. Take time to be THE MOM YOU'RE MEANT TO BE."

—KENDRA SMILEY, Professional speaker and author
of *High Wire Mom* and *Empowering Choices*,
2001 Illinois Mother of the Year

"This book is a great resource for moms. It's like sitting down with a wise and godly woman with her arm around your shoulder sharing her wisdom. Thanks, Cheri, for taking the time to write it all down!"

—DENISE GLENN, Founder, MotherWise Ministries

"Pull up a chair, pour yourself a cup of coffee, and get ready to be encouraged. *The Mom You're Meant to Be* offers a refreshing, guilt-free, and practical approach to motherhood from God's perspective. Cheri Fuller has done it again. Let her help you relax, rely on God, and actually enjoy being a mom while you're living through those active parenting years. A must read!"

—CLAUDIA & DAVID ARP, Authors of *Answering the
Eight Cries of the Spirited Child* and *10 Great Dates*

The Mom
You're Meant to Be

FOCUS ON THE FAMILY®

The Mom You're Meant to Be

Loving Your Kids
While Leaning on God

Cheri Fuller

Tyndale House Publishers, Inc.
Wheaton, Illinois

ISBN: 1-58997-132-9

A Focus on the Family book published by
Tyndale House Publishers, Wheaton, Illinois 60189

All Scripture quotations, unless otherwise indicated, are taken from the *Holy Bible,
New International Version*®. NIV®. Copyright © 1973, 1978, 1984 by International
Bible Society. Used by permission of Zondervan Publishing House. All rights reserved.
Scripture quotations marked (NKJV) are taken from the *New King James Version*.
Copyright © 1982 by Thomas Nelson, Inc. Used by permission. All rights reserved.
Scripture quotations marked (NASB) are taken from the *New American Standard
Bible*®. Copyright the Lockman Foundation 1960, 1962, 1963, 1968, 1971, 1972,
1973, 1975, 1977, 1995. Used by permission. (www.Lockman.org). Scripture quota-
tions marked ESV are from The Holy Bible, English Standard Version, copyright ©
2001 by Crossway Bibles, a division of Good News Publishers. Used by permission.
All rights reserved.

Focus on the Family books are available at special quantity discounts when purchased
in bulk by corporations, organizations, churches, or groups. Special imprints, messages, and excerpts can be produced to meet your needs. For more information, contact: Resource Sales Group, Focus on the Family, 8605 Explorer Drive, Colorado
Springs, CO 80920; or phone (800) 932-9123.

Editors: Kathy Davis and Cheri Rayburn
Cover Design: Lauren Swihart
Cover Photos: Photodisc

Library of Congress Cataloging-in-Publication Data
Fuller, Cheri.
  The mom you're meant to be: loving your kids while leaning on God /
Cheri Fuller.
        p. cm.
Includes bibliographical references.
  ISBN 1-58997-132-9
      1. Mothers—Religious life. 2. Parenting—Religious aspects—Christianity. I. Title.
BV 4529.18 .F85 2003
248.8'45—dc21

                                                                    2002153964

Printed in the United States of America
3 4 5 6 7 8 9 / 09 08 07 06 05 04

Also by Cheri Fuller

When Teens Pray
When Children Pray
When Families Pray
When Mothers Pray
When Couples Pray
The Fragrance of Kindnesses
My Wish for You: Blessings for Daughters
Opening Your Child's Spiritual Windows
Opening Your Child's Nine Learning Windows
Quiet Whispers from God's Heart for Women
Trading Your Worry for Wonder
21 Days to Helping Your Child Learn
Teaching Your Child to Write
Motherhood 101
Christmas Treasures of the Heart
Unlocking Your Child's Learning Potential
365 Ways to Develop Values in Your Child
365 Ways to Help Your Child Learn and Achieve
365 Ways to Build Your Child's Self-Esteem
How to Grow a Young Music Lover
Home Business Happiness
Helping Your Child Succeed in Public School
A Mother's Book of Wit and Wisdom
Extraordinary Kids: Nurturing and Championing Your Child with Special Needs
Motivating Your Kids from Crayons to Career
HomeLife: The Key to Your Child's Success at School
Creating Christmas Memories: Family Traditions for a Lifetime

In memory of Mama

In gratitude to Mimi

Acknowledgments

Special thanks:

- To Mark Maddox, my editor Kathy Davis, Bonnie Schulte, Allison James, Focus on the Family, and Tyndale Publishers for sharing my vision for this book and all their efforts to make it the book it needed to be! It is a joy to partner with you in ministering to the hearts of moms.
- To mothers who've encouraged and mentored me along my journey: Patty Johnston, Flo Perkins, Billie Milburn and especially my mom and mother-in-law, Joan, for all the wonderful wisdom, prayers, support, and love.
- To my agent and friend Greg Johnson who I greatly appreciate.
- To my prayer partners and sisters in Christ, Peggy Stewart and Jo Hayes—how grateful I am for our friendship and your faithful intercession.
- To three special moms who do a wonderful job of nurturing our five grandchildren—Tiffany, Maggie, and Alison. I learn so much from you and your kids!
- To my ever-faithful, always supportive, praying husband, Holmes—It has been so much fun to do parenting and now grandparenting with you!
- To you, the reader, for opening your heart to mine.

Table of Contents

The Mom You're Meant to Be

"Can you cook . . . that is, besides Kraft Macaroni & Cheese?" my aunt asked me one Saturday only a few months before my wedding. It was not a rhetorical question. She knew I'd spent my childhood outside playing instead of in the kitchen learning to cook with Mama.

"Well, no, but just give me some recipes and I can learn!" I replied.

After the wedding, I tucked my trusty wooden recipe box of "no-fail" casserole dishes under my arm and I was ready to tackle this new challenge with recipes for meaty macaroni, mushroom soup stroganoff, and chili stew. But a few of the recipes weren't as "no-fail" as I'd thought—as I found out one night when the whole house began to have a strange odor after the casserole of the day began to bake. My husband insisted we chuck the entrée, open the windows to air out the duplex, and go out for hamburgers.

Little by little, though, I did learn some cooking skills. I'm not a gourmet cook, but I've managed to feed a family of five.

Many of us approach parenting the way I approached cooking.

We're trying to find our way, or perhaps have been parenting a while and have lost our way, so we look for a formula—something concrete and structured that we hope might be the ideal parenting system. But through my years as a mom of children now ages 26, 28 and 31, I've found that the way isn't a formula. Instead, it's connecting with God's heart and with our kids' hearts. As we do, He will lead us and grow us into the moms we're meant to be and the parents our children need.

While there is no one recipe for perfect, foolproof parenting, there's a lot to be gleaned from reading books on child development that give you ideas and suggestions and help you understand the needs of your children as they change and grow. But you should not allow one parenting book or program to overrule your own judgment, silence your own heart response to your child, or leave out how God personally may instruct you concerning your child.

God promises wisdom when you're fresh out of it. He offers hope and comfort when you're discouraged. His joy can give you the strength you need to minister to your family—not just to survive, but to thrive and even *enjoy* the season you and your children are in. Jesus wants not only to walk alongside you in your mothering journey, but to *live through you*. And that's one of the main themes of this book—how you can love your kids while you lean on God.

While being a mom is a great privilege and gift, it's also an awesome challenge—and the biggest responsibility you'll ever face! That's why you can't do it in your own strength, but by depending on the Lord.

Besides fun things like playing at the park with our kids, cheering from the stands in a winning game, cuddling a little one's soft baby face next to yours as you rock him to sleep, or taking photos on birthdays, one of my favorite aspects of mothering is the great spiritual growth potential.

You see, being a mom gives you lots of opportunities to lose your life and to choose your child's good at the expense of your own rights; for example, when it's 2:00 A.M. and your well-deserved sleep is interrupted by a little person who needs you. Or when you'd love to read a magazine, but your children are stir-crazy and want you to read them Amelia Bedelia for the fifth time. Or when you see a needed change in your child's life and as you pray about it, the Lord points out the same need in *your* life.

So you won't think I'm writing this book because I believe I have "arrived" as a mom, let me share the three prayers most often in my heart when my children were growing up. Since no one except God is a perfect parent, I often prayed *Lord, please fill the gaps between the love my kids needed today and didn't get from me, even though I was loving them the best I could.* My second prayer was *Jesus, redeem my mistakes.* Believe me, I made plenty of them, but I was encouraged that God could use even my blunders to draw my children to Himself. And finally, *Lord, help our marriage, but let it begin in me.*

I asked for His mercy and wisdom often because I knew I couldn't do this important job apart from the Lord's grace. That's because just when I got one of my kids figured out and things were in harmony, he or she was off to a new stage with a new set of challenges and reasons for me to be on my knees.

When our oldest child became a teenager I remember my husband and me looking at each other with baffled expressions, saying, *Nothing prepared us for this!* Then after the ups and downs of high school, we adapted to the empty nest. When our kids graduated from college and got married, I faced an entirely new season: being a mother-in-law. (I'm still learning about this one!) Then came a delightful new role as grandma. Maybe these ever-changing seasons of motherhood are God's way of continually drawing us to depend on Him and not ourselves.

As mothers, we come in different colors, are from unique

backgrounds, and live in different parts of the world. But we have a lot in common: We are all working mothers from the minute we leave the delivery room because, as Leslie Parrott says, "[Mothering] depletes, expends, and burns up more time and energy than any other human activity I've encountered. It's a job that never stops. Twenty-four hours a day, seven days a week, a mom is on call to feed, clean, play, and care for her little one."[1] And that's just the first year!

As moms, we want to protect our children. We want the very best for them as we help develop their gifts and talents. We want them to become all they are meant to be! And as Christian mothers, we want our children to know and love Jesus and experience how much He loves them.

In the chapters ahead you won't find ironclad feeding formulas or ways to structure your newborn's schedule so you can get uninterrupted sleep. What you *will* find are matters of a mother's heart and reflections on becoming the mom you're meant to be— like throwing away the cookie cutter and appreciating each child's individuality; not being smug; finding a mentor mom to help you along; developing a heart for your home; and not putting off joy so you can really *enjoy* this brief season of mothering.

You'll also discover practical suggestions for making memories, building your child's faith, praying for your child in the midst of a busy life, and moving your body so you'll have enough energy to keep up with your kids and to meet the challenges of each day. You'll find some secrets to effective mothering, such as living out of a sense that people are more important than things, finding words that work to communicate with your kids, and finding creative ways to connect with your children on their turf. Plus there's wisdom from Scripture, from mothers who've gone before you, and a lot of hope, encouragement, and inspiration along the way.

My prayer is that this book will help you find a new joy in whatever season of mothering you're experiencing—because there's so much fun to be had and so much to be enjoyed in the midst of kitchen floors tracked with muddy little footprints and noisy vanloads of kids you're carting around. And while each chapter has several suggestions, don't think you have to do it all. Pick one that fits where you are as a mom and try it out, and save the other ideas for a different season. You can ponder the "Question for Reflection" by journaling, praying, or talking it over with a friend or in a small moms' group.

More importantly, as you read, remember: When you get to the end of your rope, you'll find God there. Although I've often found myself fresh out of loving feelings and low on patience, I've found that as Romans 8:36-39 promises, God's love never fails. If you surrender to Him in those "end of your rope, all out of love" moments, receive His love for you, and are willing to be a conduit of His love to your children, husband, and others around you, you'll be amazed at the grace He gives you again and again to be the mom you're meant to be as you love your kids while leaning on God.

2

Throw Away the Cookie Cutter

It was a hot, sunny day, and I was watching poolside as two neighborhood four-year-olds, Jenny and Olivia, began a swimming lesson.

"Let's play the submarine game and go under the water at the count of three," their instructor, John, said after they had splashed and played around for a few minutes.

Olivia dunked her head and treaded water like a fish, did an underwater handstand, and came up smiling, while her proud mom looked on. But Jenny protested, "I don't like to get my face wet! I don't want to go under!"

"Come on, honey," her mom encouraged from the sidelines. "You can do it. Going under the water is fun."

"No, it's not! I wanna go home," Jenny wailed.

"Okay, we'll play a different game," John suggested. "London Bridge is falling down, falling down, falling down…and when we get to the end of the song, we'll all three go under."

John tried every strategy he knew, but nothing would coax Jenny to join in the submarine or any other game. Normally enthusiastic, she became tearful and anxious, and she didn't enjoy that swimming lesson or the ones that followed. After the first series of lessons was over, her mom wisely gave her a break and just let her play at the pool and go at her own pace. A few weeks later, on her own at the neighborhood pool, she gradually started dipping her face in the water. By the end of the summer, she was having as much fun as the other kids.

> No parent ever trained up his child in the way he should go without making an effort to know that child.
> —CHARLES R. SWINDOLL

Why was Olivia so happy to dive in and dunk her head while Jenny resisted? It was not that Olivia's mom did everything right and Jenny's mother didn't. It was about the two girls' unique temperaments. Olivia was a quick-to-warm-up child when faced with a new situation, whereas Jenny was slow to take to anything new—whether it was a new vegetable, a new baby-sitter, or a new activity, like dunking her head under the water. It also didn't hurt that Olivia's big sister was on the swim team and was a role model for her sister to follow. Jenny, on the other hand, was the oldest and first child in her family to take swimming lessons.

I faced this dilemma when I was a young mother. It seemed all my friends had "easy" babies who were compliant and quick to adjust to new situations. My firstborn, Justin, was determined and strong-spirited. He had a definite mind of his own, even from an early age. While he could be barrels of fun in familiar surroundings, new experiences, like mother-baby swim classes or a switch in preschools, might produce a loud protest.

Was I just a bad mother? Was I doing something wrong? I really wanted to be a good mom, to understand my baby, meet his

The Nine Characteristics[2]

- **Activity level:** Does your child love climbing, running, and large motor playing, or does he prefer less active pastimes like reading and drawing?
- **Predictability and consistency:** How predictable or unpredictable are your child's biological functions, like waking and sleeping, hunger, etc.?
- **Response to new situations:** What is her first response to new stimuli or unfamiliar situations—a new food, task, person, or classroom? Does she have a negative reaction, act anxious until she's tried it a few times, or jump in enthusiastically?
- **Flexibility and adaptability:** Does your child go with the flow and adapt if you're out and her nap has to be later? Or does she thrive on having a set structure to the day?
- **Sensitivity to sudden sounds, textures, and sensory stimuli:** Does your child startle easily, awaken to small sounds, cry the minute he's wet, or complain about his clothes irritating his skin? Or does it take more noise and discomfort before he reacts?
- **Positive or negative mood:** Some babies wake up after nap or nighttime sleep in a happy mood while others cry and fuss on awakening. The child who has a more cheerful temperament will likely be the one who sees the cup as "half full" while the fussier child may see the cup as "half empty."
- **High-intensity or low-intensity emotions:** Is your child easygoing about her emotions, or does she protest and cry when frustrated or sad?
- **Easily distracted or highly focused:** Does your baby want his bottle (or, later, want to finish his game) and can't be distracted from that goal? Then he's probably a focused rather than easily distracted child.
- **Attention span and persistence level:** Does your child have a long attention span and keep persevering when working on a puzzle until it's completed, or does she give up when frustrated?

needs, and keep my wits about me. But I was puzzled about how to do that.

Fortunately around this time, I found a book written by two wise child psychiatrists, Drs. Stella Chess and Alexander Thomas, called *Know Your Child*. When I saw the title on the bookshelf, I thought, *That's just what I need! I want to know and understand my child.* In the book, Chess and Thomas report findings from their 25-year study of people from infancy to adulthood. From birth onward, they explain, individuals vary in their behavior and their reactions to different life experiences. These variations indicate specific temperamental differences (see box). In each category, the authors rate individuals as mild or intense, high or low, quick or slow.

One of the most important things I discovered in this book is the term "goodness of fit" or "attunement." More important than children having "ideal" characteristics—such as adaptability and compliance—that make them easy to deal with is the "fit" that grows between parent and child. For example, what demands and expectations do I have for my child? What reactions does my child's behavior create in me? And what reactions does *my* behavior create in him? Do I accept, enjoy, and delight in my child, or am I continually frustrated or disappointed with his behavior?

> As parents affirm each child's uniqueness, the children will find it easier to believe that God accepts them just as they are.
> —NORM WRIGHT

A few years later, I learned about children's different intelligence types and learning styles (or ways of processing the information they need to learn). This information was a godsend for me. It helped me better understand, accept, and enjoy the wonderful gift of our firstborn son, then a few years later, his brother and sister. I began to realize that some of the things we were experiencing were more about differences in temperament between him and me or between him and my friends' kids. He was merely responding to experiences from his unique temperament and personality or, you might say, the way God had wired him.

The more I understood about our little one's emotional makeup, the more accepting I was of his emotions and grateful for his individuality. I was more patient with his responses to swim class (he became an excellent swimmer, by the way). Because he was determined and persistent, I realized I needed to major on the majors, instead of the minors, in discipline issues (i.e., being firm on a few issues instead of enforcing many rules and saying "no" all the time).

> For you formed my inward parts; you knitted me together in my mother's womb. I praise you, for I am fearfully and wonderfully made. Wonderful are your works; my soul knows it very well.
>
> —Psalm 139:13-14, ESV

When I stopped comparing him to the "compliant kids," I began to find ways to encourage his gifts and strengths. I saw his energy and persistence as traits that would be helpful when he faced challenges. (And truly, they are some of the strengths that contribute to the marvelous, successful adult he is today.) As I embraced his uniqueness, the "goodness of fit" between my son and me grew into a wonderful relationship that has lasted.

Our second child, Chris, was completely different—of course! And Alison, number three, was a whole new challenge and joy. Each of them has a distinct learning style. Justin's strength is auditory, Chris's more visual, and Alison's kinesthetic and visual. They each have different intelligence strengths and talents, too—one communication, teaching, leadership, and people skills; one analytical, spatial, musical, and art talent; another musical, language, and creative gifts. Each one is precious in his or her own way, fearfully and wonderfully made by our Creator, but definitely unique!

I figure God doesn't want us to rest on our laurels. Just when we've figured out one of our kids, He gives us another that baffles us completely. I think it's His way of keeping us on our toes (and knees). And besides, think how boring it would be if each of your children had the same temperament, interests, and gifts.

Here are some ways to throw away the cookie-cutter approach and get a handle on your child's uniqueness. As you review the lists with their clues to temperament, learning style, and intelligence type then consider the suggestions below, keep in mind this isn't a labeling exercise or a one-pronged approach to understanding your child. But looking at the characteristics will help you gain a big picture of your child's individuality.

Recognize each of your children's uniqueness. No two kids are alike, and to compare them or treat them alike can cause problems:

Learning Style

Imagine you're reading aloud from a book with the repeated refrain "and the rabbit went hop, hop, hop." Does your child:

- Come up close, perhaps insisting on being on your lap, to see the pictures? This is a sign of a visual learner.
- Mimic the words of the refrain or interrupt to talk about the story? This is a sign of an auditory learner.
- Move around and do what the refrain says—hop, hop, hop? This is a sign of a kinesthetic learner.

I wish he were organized like his big sister. I wish she made high grades like Mary's daughter. I wish the twins were athletic like the rest of the family. As John Drescher says, "Continual comparison builds inferiority feelings which harm personality development."[3] Comparison also causes kids to feel unaccepted for who they are. Instead of comparing, recognize and celebrate each of your kids' different God-given abilities, gifts, and personalities.

Look for the silver lining. Be aware that often what looks like a negative trait in childhood can become a terrific strength in adulthood. For example, argumentative kids usually possess an analytical talent that can help them become a successful scientist, doctor, or engineer. Bossiness in childhood is a key marker for leadership, which means your bossy child may be the future CEO of a corporation. The emotional or melancholy child can develop into an artist or actor. As an adult, the very active kid who ran his mom ragged has great energy for tasks and challenges.

Different Kinds of Smart

- **The Musical Child** is always singing a song (usually, right on pitch) or moving to a beat. He easily remembers tone, rhythm, and melody.
- **The People Smart Child** is a social butterfly, loves to be with a group playing and taking the lead, and has great communication skills.
- **The Body Smart Child** has extra energy and loves sports. She remembers songs with body movements the best.
- **The Spatially Smart Child** can look at directions in a LEGO set and put the whole project together. He enjoys drawing, solving puzzles and mazes, and designing things.
- **The Math Smart Child** is always sorting, classifying, sequencing objects, and analyzing things.
- **The Verbally Smart Child** loves word play, telling stories, and listening to books being read. She has an uncanny memory for words.

Watch, look, and listen. Turn the TV off and tune in to your child on a regular basis. Some of the best advice Chuck Swindoll has for parents is to be a student of their children. "Watch them at play. Listen to them in conversation. Some of it will crack you up. They are so funny…. You will observe other things you've never noticed before. Your mouth will drop open as you say, 'I had not realized what a need there was there.'" Then pray for a spirit of wisdom and revelation (see Colossians 1:9-12) to see your children's hearts and personalities from the Lord's perspective, to discover what motivates them, and to know how best to nurture and guide them.

QUESTION FOR REFLECTION

What do you love most about each of your children, and what do you find most frustrating? From the lists you've written, what are some unique things about each of your kids? Thank God for all of these things.

3

Don't Put Off Joy

"When my little girl gets potty trained, then it's all going to smooth out…and when I lose the extra weight I gained in pregnancy, I'm going to be so much happier," said the young mother who sat next to me at a luncheon I spoke at recently.

"When my son starts school on a full-day basis, then finally I'll get something done. With half-day kindergarten, I just get him dropped off and it's time to go pick him up. He's a bit difficult at this stage and, frankly, I'm exhausted," said another young woman next to her.

If you're like these two moms and so many others, you often find yourself thinking that you'll experience joy when…

- the finances aren't so tight and you have more money in your checking account;
- your prodigal teen turns around, starts loving God and going to youth group, and makes better grades and choices;
- your baby's teeth come in and she starts sleeping all night, letting you get some much-needed rest;
- or your husband's not so stressed.

The list of "whens and ifs" is endless, and these are all good goals. But if you stake your joy on "whens and ifs," you will find yourself perpetually frustrated, missing out on the joys and blessings God has for you in each season of life, even those that are difficult and filled with unfinished projects, teething babies, toddlers refusing to be potty trained, or challenging teens.

One thing for sure, the season you are in now—whether pregnancy, caring for babies or preschoolers, or parenting teens—will soon be gone.

Throughout Scripture, God reminds us that life is short and we can't count on what will happen tomorrow. For example, James 4:14 says, "Why, you do not even know what will happen tomorrow. What is your life? You are a mist that appears for a little while and then vanishes." Psalm 90:10 says, "For [the years] quickly pass, and we fly away."

This is the day the LORD has made; let us rejoice and be glad in it.

—PSALM 118:24

We can't make our years go any more slowly or control their circumstances (such as the baby's teeth coming in or our teenager's heart finally turning to God). But we can choose our attitude and find that there's a lot of joy to be had right where we are if we look for it.

Here are some ways to not put off joy:

Make room for fun and for things you and your kids really enjoy. I think parenthood is a great excuse to go to the park, ride bikes, and play baseball like you did when you were young. What's fun for your family might be going to the zoo or having a picnic. Maybe you enjoy going to the library for story times and puppet shows. Even if it's rainy, you can invite another mother and her children over for lunch and let your kids help you make a special treat—like "Ants on a Log" (raisins on a banana) or "Happy Face Pear Salad" (half a canned pear with a dot of mayonnaise and raisins to make a happy face).

Take advantage of seasonal joys. There is something in every season to enjoy: picking strawberries and camping out in the backyard in summer, visiting a local pumpkin patch for that perfect pumpkin in the fall, baking gingerbread cookies and drinking hot chocolate in the winter. In the spring, when smells and colors seem more vivid after the long winter, take "smelly walks" with your kids. Just stroll around the block and have them name all the things they can smell. For a "color walk," choose a color for the day—for instance, red—and during your walk, have the kids point out all the red things they see.

There is not one blade of grass, there is no color in this world that is not intended to make us rejoice.

—JOHN CALVIN

Find joy...even when your kids are sick. From time to time, when your children are sick and stuck inside, you've probably felt that a dark cloud has drifted over your home. That cloud used to drift over our home when our oldest had asthma attacks or when all three children were sick at the same time—that is, until I began to see sick days as a time to fill up my kids' emotional tanks with TLC, a time to hug, fix hot apple juice, and read books together. Instead of thinking everything will be better when your children are well, try making the most of their down time.

Every day, there are miracles and things to celebrate: a purple-and-rose sunset, an e-mail from an old friend, your child's first sentence, a sticky kiss, or even a goldfinch at your bird feeder.

> Every day brings a chance for you to draw in a breath, kick off your shoes, and dance.
>
> —OPRAH WINFREY

But the best way to experience the greatest joy is just to…

Give yourself away. "The joy that you give to others is the joy that comes back to you," said a wise John Greenleaf Whittier long ago. It's still true. When we are concerned about others and how we can be a blessing to them today, when we are being God's hands and expressing His love, He fills us with an unquenchable joy.

QUESTION FOR REFLECTION

What are some everyday miracles you've experienced lately? What are three things you really gain a lot of joy from doing? (Pick one and make time to do it this week.)

4

Never Be Too Smug

One cold Thursday afternoon, I rushed into the Mothers' Day Out room at the church to pick up my two-year-old, Chris. I was met by a frowning teacher.

"Your son bit one of the children," she said, giving me and my toddler a disapproving stare. Her tone suggested that I had something to do with this bad behavior and that it would surely lead Chris to a life of crime.

"I am so sorry," I said, taking Christopher's little hand and gathering up his diaper bag and coat to leave. I felt terrible about the incident, but the other child and his mom had already left, so I couldn't apologize to them.

Chris was my youngest son. He was such a happy toddler that people in public often stopped us to say what a good baby he was! Sunday school teachers loved having him in their classes. Neighbors were warmed by his smile. My son.

While this wasn't the only time one of my children exhibited less-than-perfect behavior, it did teach me a good lesson (one that I had many opportunities to practice as my three kids progressed through childhood and the rough waters of adolescence)—never be too smug!

Why? Because we all make mistakes. Because God loves a humble heart. And because the truth is, we never know what our precious little child or teenager is going to do next. While you can take your kids to church and do everything possible to raise them right, you can't always keep your teen from rebelling, failing a class, or making a bad decision. While you can teach good manners and encourage kindness, you can't control their behavior or make them do the right thing.

Now in the case of my toddler's biting blunder, I don't know what sparked it. But I was rehearsing possible reasons as I walked to the car…it's his first time at this Mothers' Day Out, he didn't know any of the kids, maybe he got tired of being pushed around by the bigger kids. Perhaps my usually cooperative, good-natured Chris was just having a bad day. Of course, I scolded him and explained he wasn't to bite anyone. Fortunately, this was an isolated case, not the beginning of a pattern of hostile behavior!

But the truth is, as moms, we must never be too smug. The dictionary defines *smug* as "highly self-satisfied, complacent, scrupulously correct." The Bible lumps it together with pride. And you know what Proverbs says about pride…it comes before a fall.

> We can be humble only when we know that we are God's children, of infinite value and eternally loved.
>
> —MADELEINE L'ENGLE

How do you know you've gotten smug about your mothering? Here are two telltale clues:

Critical thoughts creep into your mind when you see other less-than-perfect kids. Another mom's kids at the grocery store are begging for something, wailing, making a scene. She's embarrassed, drops things, and finally yells at the children. You think, *That'll never happen to me. My kids would never do that.*

Or your teen is at church every time the doors open and was just elected president of the youth group. Your friend's daughter can't be dragged to the youth events. In fact, she's running around with the wild crowd at school. You think, *If her parents just read devotions aloud at breakfast or went to more Bible studies or sent the kids to Christian schools like we do, she'd be more interested in spiritual things.* Oops, smugness is lurking somewhere in your attitude.

> Therefore, as God's chosen people, holy and dearly loved, clothe yourselves with compassion, kindness, humility, gentleness and patience.
>
> —COLOSSIANS 3:12

There's no room for improvement, new ideas, or advice from anyone else. For example, if you think you've cornered the market on great parenting because you home school and believe all our country's problems would be solved if everyone else did too, you might be a little smug. If you have followed some parenting formula that has worked for you, are a diligent disciplinarian, and don't value other parenting styles, watch out. If you change the subject or tune out when an older mom or one who does things differently shares her experience with you, smugness might be the cause. I have found that when we lose our "teachable-ness," we are missing out on wisdom that we are going to need for the journey ahead.

If you feel smugness has crept into your attitude, or if you want to avoid it, here are some tips:

Walk in humility and gratefulness, no matter how well your kids behave, how high their grades are, or how fast their spiritual growth is progressing. This is biblical. And besides, if your kids are doing great at the moment (or turn out great in the end), it's more about God's grace than expert parenting skills. Thank Him!

Value and respect other ways of mothering, schooling, and operating as a family, especially if it's different from your way of doing things. Don't compare yourself to other moms—you'll end up feeling either superior or inferior. Avoid the comparison trap by acknowledging that God has made each family for different purposes and callings. Let Him be God, and strive to be a supporter and cheerleader for other moms!

Be compassionate instead of judgmental. Send a little prayer heavenward for that mom in the grocery store whose kids are going ballistic. Instead of judging the brokenhearted mother whose teen is more interested in partying and alcohol than youth group, put an arm around her and pray with her for her son or daughter.

> Wisdom is oftentimes nearer when we stoop than when we soar.
> —WILLIAM WORDSWORTH

Avoid if-then thinking, such as… *If* I raise my children according to God's ways, *if* I always take them to church and don't allow them to (you name it), *if* I require them to go to Christian camp every summer, *then* they will turn out exactly the way I want them to. Of course, you hope and pray they will turn out wonderfully well, and you do your part to be the best mom and nurture and train them in right paths, but remember, your kids have free choice and "if-then" thinking can set you up for disappointment.

QUESTION FOR REFLECTION

How can you be supportive and give grace to a mom who is struggling with her child's misbehavior or some other difficult aspect of her family life?

5

People Are More Important Than Things

Lisa, a young mother of two, set her sights on transforming an antique, six-by-four-foot farmhouse table that had been in the family for years. It would mean stripping the piece of its seven layers of paint, re-staining it, and putting on several coats of polyurethane. But she was ready for the task.

With grandma helping with the kids, Lisa began Monday morning and got as far as stripping the top when other duties called her away. All day Tuesday was spent stripping with a loud power stripper, and by the end of the day, her muscles were shaking with fatigue. Wednesday she labored in 104-degree heat in the garage, sanding and staining the table.

Early Thursday morning, Lisa applied the first coat of polyurethane. Friday she put on coats number two and three. On Saturday she got out to the garage early because she could hardly wait to put the final coat of polyurethane on this absolutely gorgeous table. A friend who dropped by told Lisa her handiwork was stunning; the tabletop looked like it had glass on it because she could see her reflection. For 15 minutes, Lisa basked in the glow of that comment and just stood back and admired all she'd accomplished that week. She couldn't wait for the table to be sitting in her kitchen in a few days, her family enjoying a meal on it.

When another friend dropped by and told her how beautiful the table was, Lisa was busy cleaning up rags and brushes. As she was talking with her friend, she heard, "Look, Mommy, I can help you!"

Her little Samantha, four years old, had gone into the storage room, picked up the paintbrush that had been soaking in gasoline, and was sloshing it enthusiastically across the top of that perfectly smooth table. "See how I'm helping you with the table, Mommy!"

Lisa felt every muscle in her body go limp. She froze in shock. The only words that would come out of her mouth were "Ohhhh, noooooo!" All those hours of work in the heat. All that stripping, sanding, painting—all ruined. She wanted to yell, "Samantha, how could you do this? You know how hard Mommy has worked on this! Why did you do it?" But she held the words back and took a deep breath.

> But we were gentle among you, like a mother caring for her little children.
>
> —1 THESSALONIANS 2:7

Samantha's smile turned into a very sad expression as she suddenly realized she wasn't really helping her mommy. Lisa tried to explain that the brush didn't have paint on it but a chemical that eats through paint. She assured her daughter, "It's going to be okay, honey. Let me think for a minute. Why don't you go to your room and I'll come up soon." This exhausted mom needed a few minutes alone to calm down and think.

Later when they talked, Lisa told Samantha that she could fix the table and they'd love it no matter how it turned out. Lisa called her dad and he told her what to do to redeem the table. But it took four more long, hot days of working to undo the damage and repair the finish.

The table now sits in Lisa's kitchen with burn marks from the stripper. (Using it twice burned the table's surface in places.) Its flaws are a constant reminder to Lisa that people are more important than things.

Is the table as perfect as the first time she refinished it? No. But is it really that important? No. Lisa knows it is just a table and her daughter is a wonderful creation of God, with a radiance and shine of Christ in her that truly is like glass. You can see through her a reflection of Jesus…now *that* is what truly matters.

Lisa could have wounded Samantha's spirit that day if she'd been more concerned about the less-than-perfect table than her daughter's heart. But long before this mishap, she'd made the decision that people are more important than things, and that included antique tables.

> A sparkling house is a fine thing if the children aren't robbed of their luster in keeping it that way.
>
> —MARCELENE COX

Our culture encourages us to value money, possessions, a picture-perfect house, and gourmet meals above spending time with our kids. But when you focus on keeping a perfect house, keeping up appearances, and making everything look "right" (including the kids), your perspective gets skewed.

God sometimes brings an unlikely person into your life to help you rearrange your priorities. One day, a woman I know was delivering something to her friend Karen. When she knocked on the door, there was no answer, so she just went into the house. She lived in a small town where people felt safe leaving their doors unlocked. When she entered, she saw piles of laundry, unwashed dishes, and a general mess. Her first thought was, *Why isn't Karen here taking care of things? My house is sparkling at all times.*

> Remember what counts. Little things and little people weigh heavily in the scales of heaven. Remember what it was like to be this size when wonder came so easily. Remember how it felt to always be looking up.
>
> —DEENA LEE WILSON

When she looked out into the backyard, she saw Karen with her five small children gathered around her in a tight circle. They were very excited about what they were doing. She went out and discovered that Karen and her kids were watching a trail of ants. That day changed this woman's mind forever about her priorities because she realized that if Karen had been inside doing the laundry and cleaning the house, she and her children would have missed the ants.

QUESTION FOR REFLECTION

What's most important to you? Is there a "trail of ants" your kids are missing out on today because you are too busy keeping a perfect home?

6

Follow the Leader

Jordan put her hands on her hips, pointed her finger, and said, "You will just have to go to time out!" She was reprimanding her mom, who had lost her temper when the dog got out, making her chase him around the neighborhood. Kathy laughed as she realized how much her daughter sounded just like she did.

Most of us have seen our children do mirror-image imitations of things we've said or done. As a wise older mom once told me, "Kids seldom misquote you. They more often repeat word for word what you shouldn't have said."

But the good news is that the very way our kids watch us and imitate what we do can be a powerful tool for motivating them in positive ways.

"I want my kids to be motivated. I want them to like learning, not to look at it as drudgery!" say countless moms in groups I've spoken to. In fact, you have within you the best motivator of all—your position as a role model.

"Actions speak louder than words," my dad always said, and he was right. Words are important, but actions impact our children even more and are more often imitated by them. Like it or not, kids play "Follow the Leader," and for many years we—as moms and dads—are the leaders. Our children mirror our attitudes and habits in so many areas.

The dictionary defines *model* as "a person or thing which is regarded as a standard of excellence to be imitated." You and I may not feel like a standard of excellence, but kids are careful observers of what we do. Watching adults is the primary way kids learn about acceptable attitudes and behaviors. Whatever they see us do, they assume is okay for them to do too. They internalize what we do as the values they will live by.

Studies about the use of seat belts, tobacco, alcohol, and drugs show that the main factor determining whether kids say "yes" or "no" is their parents' example, especially their moms'.

For example, one survey showed that mothers have the greatest influence on getting children to wear seat belts in cars. More than TV or school campaigns featuring sports heroes, movie stars, or police officers, seeing Mom buckle up has a powerful effect on kids' safety habits. The same principle holds true for smoking, eating, television viewing, drinking, table manners, and language habits—children tend to do what their parents do, not what they say.

> Children are born mimics. They behave like their parents despite all our efforts to teach them manners.
>
> —UNKNOWN

Don't get me wrong, dad also has a big impact on the kids' desire to learn and achieve, but mom is usually the point person when it comes to school involvement, helping with homework, and learning. And mothers tend to spend the most time with the kids. This is both a happy and a scary thought—such a big responsibility we moms have!

But let's think about it positively for a moment and how being a positive role model can help your children become motivated learners. Motivation happens to kids with parents who are intellectually alive and show excitement over the world of books, ideas, and numbers—it's contagious, say experts.

A child will catch a love of learning from a mom who likes to find things out, who is curious herself, who enjoys learning for its own sake, who adds to her store of knowledge simply because it's fun. It's not that hard, either, to be a good example in this way. Try these suggestions:

Keep learning. If you don't know something—like how to grow cactus or make grapevine wreaths, for example—head for the library with your child. Let him see you check out the computerized card catalog, ask the library staff for help, and find the resources. If you take a workshop at a hobby store or local community college, your actions motivate your child to dig for useful information on things that interest him. Besides, learning something new keeps our brains sharp, which we need if we're going to keep up with our kids as they grow!

One mother can achieve more than a hundred teachers.

—JEWISH PROVERB

Model writing and reading. When you write a letter to a great-aunt, thank-you notes, or a letter of complaint to a business, let your kids see what you're doing. They will understand the usefulness of writing. If you're an avid reader and spend more time reading than watching TV, if your kids hear you laugh as you read the Sunday comics or find you enjoying a novel, then they are more likely to catch the magic of reading. And if they see you reading the Bible and spending time with God as a regular part of your day, then they'll know how important God and His word are. Your actions can be the best sermon of all.

Admit your mistakes. Even in your mistakes, you can be a good role model! When you're willing to admit your errors, learn from your failures, and ask forgiveness when you hurt someone, then kids learn the value of repentance and how to handle mistakes. They tend to risk making mistakes in order to grow, knowing they have the support of parents who aren't perfect—just forgiven.

QUESTION FOR REFLECTION

What are some positive examples you can set for your children this week to build up their character or boost their motivation?

7

Teaching Your Kids to Pray

Patty, a young mother I know, was just finishing her boys' school-work for the day when the telephone rang.

"The trees near our home are on fire!" her sister Marianne yelled. "The fire department is already here. They told us to get any important paperwork and medications and get out. We only have ten minutes until the flames reach our house!" Marianne's family lived on several acres of land surrounded by dense woods, and the drought in Texas only made the fire spread more quickly.

As Marianne grabbed photo albums and ripped pictures off the walls, she pleaded, "Pray for us!"

Patty promised she would and shot an arrow prayer for God's protection of her sister's home and family as she opened the cabinet door to get the prayer chain phone numbers. *I'll get all the pray-ers I know mobilized*, she thought as she dialed the first number. As she hung up the phone to call another, Patty realized her second grader, Andrew, and his older brother, Grant, had overheard the conversation. She knew then that the chain of prayer needed to begin right there with her boys.

Patty ran for her Bible and, holding hands with Grant and Andrew, prayed with them that God would hold the fire back from her sister's house, save as many trees and as much land as possible, and give the firemen the advantage over the flames. Then she suggested Grant read Psalm 91 aloud to Andrew and pray with him while she contacted others on the prayer chain.

While making the rest of the calls, Patty could see her kids in the next room interceding for their cousins, aunt, and uncle. When their mom rejoined them, they continued praying Psalm 91 and lingered on verses 9 and 10, which say, "If you make the Most High your dwelling—even the LORD, who is my refuge—then no harm will befall you, no disaster will come near your tent." Remembering that Marianne had named her house "Crosswings" several years before, they prayed verse four, that God would cover the home with His feathers and that the family would find refuge under His wings as the angels held back the flames.

Minutes flew by as they prayed and read the verses, and before long, the phone rang again. Patty leaped to answer it, her heart racing. It was Marianne again, but this time with good news. The fire had burned eight acres and come as close as 37 footsteps from their house when it was stopped. Firefighters were still working on the embers, but the blaze was under control and their home was saved.

> All your children shall be taught by the LORD, and great shall be the peace of your children.
>
> —ISAIAH 54:13, NKJV

Patty was so glad she'd brought her boys into the circle of prayer and that they had the hands-on opportunity to go into action (instead of worrying and feeling helpless) when something bad happened. She was even happier that they had seen God's mighty response.

But it doesn't take a crisis to find reasons to pray with your children. There are plenty of everyday problems, situations, your own needs, and the needs of others to pray about together. And when prayer is your first response instead of a last resort, you help your kids learn the value of going to God with the little things as well as the big things.

When I speak on prayer, moms often ask me, "How can I teach my children to pray?" Here are some ways:

Be a pray-er yourself, and ask your kids to partner with you in prayer. Just like chicken pox or the common cold, the motivation to pray is contagious. Kids catch it from parents who talk and listen to God with their children in the spontaneous moments of living together. The most powerful teaching tool you have is to respond with the power of prayer to all of the needs, burdens, concerns, and problems you face.

Prayer is as simple as a child making known its wants to its parents.

—OSWALD CHAMBERS

Help your kids see things around them as visual aids to prompt prayer. When they see a parking spot for disabled people, they could pray for those with special needs and disabilities. If you're driving and hear a siren or see an ambulance speeding down the street, ask one of your kids to send a prayer heavenward for the emergency room workers who will treat the injured people and for safety for the ambulance drivers. And just as Patty did, bring your kids into the prayer circle when there is a problem or emergency situation you see or hear about.

Pray conversationally. Instead of saying a rote prayer over meals or formalizing prayer, speak to God as a friend. Use simple, conversational language and short sentences rather than long, flowery, formal words. Then kids will think, *I can do that* and are more apt to talk to God in their own way and know that He hears them. Encourage your children that short expressions, like *Help, God* or *Thank You, Lord*, are wonderful prayers. And give them a hands-on way to pray, like putting a globe in the middle of the dinner table and letting each child spin it and pray a short prayer of blessing for the country their hand lands on.

Ground your prayers in God's Word. Have your kids ever said, "I don't know what to say!" when you ask them to pray? Teach them how the Bible can shape their prayers. When kids learn to pray God's Word, their prayer vocabulary increases and they grow in confidence because their prayers hit the target and are right in line with God's best for their lives. Praying verses like Philippians 4:13: *Lord, thank You that I can do all things (even my hard math homework) because You give me strength* or Psalm 106:1: *Thank You, Lord! How good You are!* can jump-start their conversation with God.

> A prayer prayed from the heart of the child to the Father is never in vain.
>
> —ELISABETH ELLIOT

As you take the ordinary experiences of life and turn them into prayer moments with your kids, you'll be guiding them into a closer relationship with their heavenly Father and an invaluable source of help and grace for the rest of their lives.

QUESTION FOR REFLECTION

What is your family's greatest need? Look for a scripture that addresses that need and pray it together.

8

A Heart for Your Home

♡

In these days of fast-forward living and ever-changing mobility, it's easy for the place you live to become a pit stop instead of a home—a place to drop in and microwave something to eat or change clothes between activities, but not a place where real life happens. Sometimes we have a sense that what's happening "out there," at that place we're rushing to get to, is much more important than what's going on inside our own four walls. Then there's the whole matter of creating a home. And if you're living "temporary," that's a challenge. But even in a duplex or tiny apartment, you can bring your heart—your personality, uniqueness, and creativity—to create a home.

When Holmes and I married in 1969, we lived in a one-bedroom duplex in a shaky neighborhood in Waco, Texas. We had a very small budget: $27 a week for groceries, $115 for rent, $5 a week for gas, and little for new furniture or accessories. We had a Kmart wicker settee with an orange corduroy cushion from my parents, a lovely set of dishes, some kitchen stuff, and a little box full of recipes I couldn't wait to try out. Fortunately, the place came with a bed, dresser, and an old dining room table because we didn't have those items. We put our candlesticks (a wedding present) on the table, and Holmes made a lamp for the living room. After a few months, we saved enough to go to the flea market where we found an old architect's table for $10 to put plants on and some used frames for inexpensive art prints we had gotten at a museum.

It wouldn't make the Pottery Barn catalog, but it was home! I graded papers there at night since I taught English by day. We had friends over for spaghetti or ice cream. It was just temporary—we only lived there a year and a half. After four houses in the neighborhood were robbed, we found another little house to rent.

> Anyone can build a house. We need the Lord for the creation of a home.
>
> —JOHN HENRY JOWETT

In each place we lived, we painted, fixed up, made curtains, and put up wallpaper—creating a place to call home. When the kids came along, we refurbished a rocking chair, made a Raggedy Andy wall decoration, and painted an unfinished little dresser with bright lime green, blue, and yellow drawers (remember, it was the 1970s). We thought we'd created the cutest nursery ever!

How can you build a home, a place where your own and your family's hearts are rejuvenated, where creativity takes place, memories are made, books are read, and laughter and games are mixed in with the chores?

Surround yourself with stuff you and your spouse love, things that have meaning and depth to you, such as a treasured collection of stories, items from your favorite hobby, flowers (homegrown if you can't afford the florist's variety), family photos, a collection of shells or something else special to you, a quilt to wrap up in when you're cold.

Paint and fix up now, not later. Don't wait until you're putting your house on the market to hang wallpaper, paint, or complete those projects that would make it more livable and comfortable. And don't wait until the décor is "perfect" or until you have a bigger dining room or a new table and chairs to ask friends over for dinner. Fresh paint, homemade curtains, and photos hung on a special wall can help make a place more inviting. Do these things soon after moving in so you can really enjoy where you live right from the start, for as long as you're there. Remember, all our houses on earth are temporary, even if we own them. Our real Dwelling Place is the Lord, and when we get to heaven, we won't ever have to pack again!

> Home is not just a place you live—it's a place you grow up in.
> —CHRISTINA, AGE 8

Pray for a heart for your home. Once you have the walls painted and furniture arranged, it's easy to become so focused on your job, church, grad school, or other activities that you neglect your home and have little left to give your family. Creating a home—with a semblance of order, loveliness, warm hospitality, and cherished memories—takes the heart of someone who wants to make a home. If your heart needs some warming toward home, ask God for that desire. Ask Him for whatever is lacking— a sense of order, a bigger picture of your influence, or a mentor who can share practical tips and help you along in the area of homemaking.

Overwhelmed by the piles? As a young mother, I was secretly always hoping my fairy godmother would show up, zip around like Mr. Clean, and clean my house, especially on days when I was tired and overwhelmed by mounds of dirty diapers (we couldn't afford disposable ones), laundry, and dirty dishes. I was not a natural organizer! Elisabeth, a woman who invited us younger moms from the church to her house for a "Prayer and Share" group, had the most amazingly organized house, and I loved just peeking in her perfectly arranged drawers and cabinets. Being with her (and asking her questions) inspired me and caused me to ask God even more—*Lord, help me in this area of homemaking!*

And you know what? He did. My sweet husband also often came alongside me, pitching in and helping out. We found that what worked for us as a family (especially when I was teaching part-time and helping Holmes at his store) was doing two hours of chores on Saturday, all together. Everybody had a list, including the kids, and afterward, we went out to the park or for pizza. Find what works for you.

Simple Things that Make a Home a Refuge

- Play CDs of soothing classical or Christian music, or turn on the classical radio station as a background rather than the TV.
- Start dinner earlier in the day by making a casserole. Later, add store-bought French bread (or made-in-your-oven bread) and salad in a bag, and voilà!—a lovely meal for you and your family or even a guest. Then during the pre-dinner hour, when kids are often the crankiest, anxious for dad to come home, make it a "happy hour." Put out fresh veggies and dip, or fruit slices with cheese, and play a game.
- Ask for God's love and peace to fill your heart and home each day.

QUESTION FOR REFLECTION

What makes you feel at home? A nook for your hobby, a throw to cuddle up in for an impromptu nap, a few green plants, a basket of books? What would it take for you to "build" your home?

Ah! There is nothing like staying at home, for real comfort.

—JANE AUSTEN

9

Fingerprints on the Wall

I raced into the grocery store, eight-month-old in my arms and three-year-old in hand, to pick up Tylenol, a prescription, apple juice, and a few other groceries. I was on my way home from the doctor's office, and my "To Do" list was nowhere near done. There was dinner to cook, as well as housework and dirty diapers waiting for me at home.

I gathered up the things I needed and hit the checkout counter, impatiently waiting to get my change so I could dash out the door, when all of a sudden, an older woman came up behind. She stopped me and said, "Slow down and enjoy your boys while they're little. The time will go so fast! My two sons are now grown and live on different coasts. How I miss them and wish I could spend the day with them!"

The time didn't seem to be going fast. In fact, some days it seemed to be crawling. Those were the days when I could barely see over the stacks of dirty diapers, when I was cooped up with my children's bouts of bronchitis or ear infections, spilled milk, and whines of "Mommy!" On those days, it seemed like I hadn't talked to an adult in weeks. It didn't help that Holmes worked long hours and, since we were newcomers to the city, I didn't know any other moms.

Yet I knew the woman was right. And when I went home that day, I slowed down enough to make LEGO forts and castles with my boys then stroll them to the park to play.

Perhaps you've received similar advice from an older mom too—but it bears pondering again. Because the truth is, your kids' childhood will pass so quickly. You know they'll grow up some-day. But in reality, that day comes so soon. In the twinkling of an eye, each of your kids will be taking off for college or career. Try this little exercise: Close your eyes and picture your child strolling down the aisle with his graduating class. Decked out in cap and gown, he walks across the stage when his name is called and grasps his diploma. Then a few short months later, he piles all his stuff in his car and heads across the country for college. When that happens, you won't be thinking, *I wish I'd spent more time at the office or polishing the floors.*

> It will be gone before you know it. The fingerprints on the wall will appear higher and higher, and then suddenly they disappear.
>
> —DOROTHY EVSLIN

I remember the morning after our son Justin got married. I was getting dressed when all of a sudden, I thought I heard his distinctive, wonderful laugh coming from the front of the house. Oh, how I loved that laugh. But then with a feeling of sadness, I thought, *No, that can't be Justin. He doesn't live here anymore. He has his own place where he and Tiffany will live.* (Besides, I knew they were on their honeymoon!) But in that moment, the house seemed very quiet. Graduation photos on the piano. Toys stored in the attic. No music blaring from his room.

Perhaps your home is still filled with the footsteps of little (or big) kids that run, skip, or jump but rarely walk. Lucky you! Or you're on the verge of seeing your kids fly from the nest. Like my friend Melina told me one summer, "In two years Gib will be gone to college! I wish I could make time stop! It's moving too fast!"

You can't make time stop as life proceeds and your children grow, so what can you do to savor and enjoy the time you do have together? How can a mother make the most of those fleeting, sometimes exhausting, yet sweet years of child-rearing?

Perhaps parents would enjoy their children more if they stopped to realize the film of childhood can never be run through for a second showing.

—EVELYN NOWN

See your life in seasons. Recognize that as women, our lives change in a seasonal way and that no family situation is static. Lives and possibilities will be different five or 10 years down the road. Recognizing this truth is especially vital today because we have a tendency to think we have to do everything this year or achieve certain goals before age 30. It's also an important truth to consider when making decisions about work and finances that will impact the family.

As Brenda Hunter says, there is "world enough and time" to dream new dreams, pursue careers, and focus energies in different directions after children are raised. "We can have it all—but not all at once," she says. "And if we live each day fully, we won't look back over the terrain of our lives with emotional pain because we were inaccessible to our families while our children were at home."[4]

I met a woman recently on a plane who had raised five children as a stay-at-home mom. Afterward, she earned one master's degree in criminal justice, worked with juveniles who were in trouble with the law, and went on to earn another master's degree in psychology. When I met her, she had practiced as a marriage and family counselor for over 10 years and was more energetic than most 30-year-olds. She was pursuing goals she wanted to fulfill and was still going strong in her 60s.

> There is so little empty space. The space is scribbled on, the time has been filled. Too many activities, and people, and things… For it is not merely the trivial which clutters our lives but the important as well.
>
> —ANNE MORROW LINDBERGH

Even while you're in your active parenting years, you can develop your gifts and talents, volunteering in your child's school, home school co-op group, church, or community. There are also home businesses, flextime jobs, and other options that help a mom keep family as a priority. If you love painting, set up a corner of a room to paint. If gardening is your passion, let the yard be your canvas. If you love writing or any other creative pursuit, schedule small blocks of time to pursue your craft.

Find your own "slow-down spots of time" together. "Slow down is my best advice to young mothers," said Leonette, an older woman I once met. "We can get so involved with doing things and getting everything done that we begin to look at our children as interruptions instead of priorities," she added. Lying on a quilt looking up at the night sky's constellations, you will find that time slows down a little. Moments sitting on the edge of your child's bed to listen, encourage, and pray for her concerns are precious. So are taking time for a walk, sharing an ice cream sundae, or reading in sleeping bags by the fireplace.

> So teach us to number our days that we may get a heart of wisdom.
>
> —PSALM 90:12, ESV

Don't let yourself and your kids get so busy and overcommitted that you're constantly rushing from one place to another. A recent study showed that the main cause of tension in women's lives is too much to do and not enough time to do it, feeling like splintered fragments, going in too many directions. Instead of over-scheduling your and your children's days so that there's no lag time at all, try letting each child pick one extracurricular activity every six months just for themselves and one activity during each week to do with you and your husband.

Life is a gift. Every day is a gift. As you give your time to God each day, keep in mind what's most important. Then like the girl who spun straw into gold in the fairy tale "Rumpelstiltskin," you can use this time and see each moment turn into gold.

QUESTION FOR REFLECTION

What really matters to you? Write down what are the most important, non-negotiable things in your life. They could include…The love of husband, kids, family, and friends. The joy of knowing God. Helping a friend who has just lost her child or is in the hospital. Time to take a walk, create something, or sing a song. Making your house a place of hospitality. Teaching your kids and helping them know Jesus. Then ask yourself, *Am I using my time to do these things and attain these goals?*

10

Listen with Your Heart

♡

A mom I met at a conference shared with me about a time she was bustling in the kitchen, fixing dinner for company. Her little boy, Matt, was following her around, pulling on her skirt, trying to tell her what had happened that day at school.

"Mommy, I was on the playground and Jake ran up and hit me and I fell out of the swing, and didn't know what to do so I…"

"Oh, honey, I've gotta get dinner fixed and I'm way behind," she replied.

"Here's the picture I colored. Look!" Matt said.

"In a few minutes, when I finish this…"

He kept on talking, telling her another story. As he was wrapping it up he asked, "Are you listening, Mommy?"

"Sure, honey," his mom said as she turned off the mixer and started setting the table.

Finally, Matt stopped her. She stooped down, and they looked at each other eye to eye. He put his little hands on her cheeks and said, "But Mommy, would you listen with your face?"

Many of us are like that mother. Talking we can handle. In fact, the average woman spends one-fifth of her life talking and speaks 30,000 words a day, enough to fill 66 books of 800 pages each every year! I am right up there with the 30,000-words-a-day talkers. Listening, especially with our full attention, isn't what we do best. Sometimes we're too busy to listen or are too distracted or are feeding the baby and juggling multiple tasks.

But before long, we wonder why our kids won't talk to us (especially when they get to the pre-teen and teen years) and wish they would. What we've forgotten is that 80 percent of the communication process is listening. Somebody once said that the fact God gave us two ears and one mouth should give us a clue. But while listening is the most important aspect of communication, it's often the most neglected.

> Take a moment to listen today
> To what your children are trying to say…
> Listen to their problems
> Listen for their needs…
> Tolerate their chatter
> Amplify their laughter
> Find out what's the matter
> Find out what they're after
> But tell them that you love them
> Every single night…
> Listen today, whatever you do
> And they will come back to listen to you.
> —UNKNOWN

Becoming a better listener to my kids has been a long journey for me. I came from a family of five girls, all talkers, and a little brother who had to work hard to get a word in edgewise. When I realized how deficient I was in this area—in a way similar to Matt's mom's experience—I made listening one of my goals. I haven't arrived, but I have discovered some ways to improve:

When your child is talking, give her eye contact and pay attention to her words, feelings, and body language.

Start small. Instead of aiming to listen to your child or husband for an hour or two, start with a goal of spending five minutes a day listening to each one.

Be available to talk at odd times, day and night. And be willing to talk about sensitive subjects without overreacting. When you overreact to what your kids share, they tend to clam up and not tell you anything significant.

Ask good questions, the open-ended kind. Closed questions can be answered with a "yes" or "no" and close the door on conversation. Open-ended questions encourage thinking and communication, and they don't have a right or wrong answer. For example, instead of "How was school today?" (to which your child may reply "fine" or "okay") try "What was your favorite part of the day?" or "What was the worst thing that happened today?" Or have some fun with creative questions, like "What would it be like to have wings instead of arms? What things could you do that you can't do now?"

> The patience and the humility of the face she loved so well was a better lesson to Jo than the wisest lecture, the sharpest reproof.
>
> —LOUISA MAY ALCOTT, LITTLE WOMEN

Practice active listening. Active listening doesn't judge everything that comes out of your kids' mouths with "You shouldn't feel like that." Instead of responding, "I don't know why you're feeling so angry about not getting chosen for the team at recess," you could say, "It sounds like you're mad and hurt about not being picked for the team. I can sure understand that!" And let them know they're really heard before offering solutions for a problem.

> Everyone should be quick to listen, slow to speak and slow to become angry.
>
> —JAMES 1:19

When it's a problematic situation or conflict, silently pray for your child while she's talking. Ask God to put His thoughts in your mind and show you how to respond.

A counselor told me once that for many kids, the world can seem like a scary landscape. That's where we moms and dads should come in, to help moderate the normal, predictable fears and aches of childhood and adolescence. Sharing time, talking, and having someone listen with the heart are often the very best medicine for the struggles of growing up.

And there's a side benefit of good communication: It fosters children's learning and achievement. Research shows that students who do well on mental tests and schoolwork tend to come from homes where there is lots of open communication. When children and parents are talking and listening to each other, when kids feel safe to share ideas and feelings, intellectual growth is stimulated, and those children grow to be more curious, motivated, and enthusiastic about learning.

QUESTION FOR REFLECTION

How well were you listened to when you were a child? Are you more of a talker or listener? If you have more than one child, how do you relate to their different communication styles and stages? Which one of the suggestions above could you use to tune in and listen with your heart?

11

Cultivating Friendships with Moms

We had just moved to Oklahoma City with our three children, the boys both under five years old and three-week-old baby Alison in my arms. It was a few weeks before Christmas. With no family or friends in the area, I busied myself unpacking boxes and trying to decorate the house between feedings, diaper changing, and housework. All three children had just come through a bout with bronchitis, and cabin fever had set in. Cranky and bored, they longed to get out and play with kids in the neighborhood, but we didn't know anyone. They were tired of hearing me read the same books, thinking Christmas would never come and the grandparents would never get there!

As for me, I was feeling isolated and a little blue in the long days and nights my husband was working at the retail store across town. The last neighborhood we'd lived in, in Tulsa, was made up mostly of older people and working women with not one other stay-at-home mom, so I was way overdue for adult companionship. It was holiday time, but we didn't have any gatherings to go to. I was still trying to find my way to the doctor's office, grocery store, and discount center without getting lost. *If there just were someone to call, or if I knew somebody in the neighborhood who had kids too.* I was so lonesome I could cry.

Suddenly, there was a knock at my door. A mother who looked about my age smiled and held out a handmade invitation to her neighborhood Christmas coffee that Saturday. With two little ones in tow, she said, "Bring your children, too, and cookies or bread. Join us if you have time."

> A true friend is one who knows all about you and likes you anyway.
>
> —CHRISTI MARY WARNER

If I had time! I couldn't wait for Saturday. As a newcomer, I found that coffee to be the highlight of my first holiday season in a strange new city. The country-print-covered table was filled with the cookies, coffee rings, and loaves of warm nut bread that each woman had brought. The smell of hot cider laced the room as four other mothers and I sat around the fireplace and talked about our lives, where we came from, and about our kids. That gave us a lot to talk about—among us there were 14 children!

Through the window I could see the kids bundled up, playing in the backyard. As we chatted, I suggested that we start a neighborhood play group so they—and we moms—could get to know each other better and have some time out of the house during the winter. My loneliness gradually began to dissipate as I got to know these new friends, taking stroller rides, going to the park, or having peanut butter sandwich lunches together with our kids. Oh, the joy of friends!

I've found it's hard to be the mom you were meant to be when you're lonely and isolated. We were meant for relationship, not to be Lone Ranger moms. We function best when we have someone to share the joys, struggles, and burdens of mothering—someone to laugh with about the funny things that our kids do, or to have coffee or go on outings with. A friend can quiet your fears, pray for you, and walk beside you in the journey of motherhood. Even wonderful, close relationships with husbands and children don't eliminate our need for friendships with other women. In fact, when you have kids, you *really* need friends. And it's often because of those friendships that we are able to give our best selves to those closest to us.

> Remember, the greatest gift is not found in a store nor under a tree, but in the hearts of true friends.
>
> —CINDY LEW

Without support or encouragement, things can seem over-whelming, like in my friend Jan's case. Overnight she became the mother of three children ages 8, 12, and 14 when at age 33, she married their dad, a widower. After the honeymoon, there were all kinds of challenges—cooking, laundry, and dishes for five instead of one, feeling like a stranger in her own home, trying to corral three strong-willed kids who'd been doing their own thing for a while. She felt so alone and often didn't know if she was doing the right thing regarding the children. Finally, she called Sheryl, a friend from church. Through their conversations, Jan began to see the heart of matters so she could respond instead of just react. An older mom who'd already raised two teenagers also encouraged her along and gave her advice when needed.

Maybe, like me or like Jan, you've had some lonely times as a mom. Perhaps you've moved or your neighborhood doesn't have a lot of moms your age. Or maybe your life has gotten so busy with tasks, responsibilities, and hauling kids around that you haven't had time for friendship with other women. You don't have to feel like an island in a sea of diapers or soccer balls. There are moms out there who need friends as much as you do. Here's how to find them:

Start or attend a MomTime group. MomTime is a ministry started by author, actress, and home-schooling mom Lisa Whelchel to give moms uninterrupted time with other mothers. The four F's of MomTime are Food, Faith, Fellowship, and Fun. For information about MomTime, log onto www.MomTime.com. To find out how to start a MomTime group, pick up a MomTime kit in your Christian bookstore or call 1-800-AFAMILY. (The MomTime Website and kit will be available fall 2003.)

Attend a Hearts at Home conference or one of their Moms Mornings Out groups. Hearts at Home provides resources, conferences, encouragement, and connection for moms at all stages of life. Visit www.hearts-at-home.org for more information.

Attend a MotherWise group. MotherWise is a ministry that combines Bible study, prayer circle, and mentoring/mothering skill groups. It has become a lifeline for many moms through groups that provide support, friendship, and sound Bible studies specifically on mothering. The MotherWise Website, *www.motherwise.org*, has a Group Finder to help you locate a group in your area.

Start a Girls' Night Out. Molly, Bethany, and Brook are three young mothers who were busy caring for their kids and got very few breaks. So they decided to plan a monthly Girls' Night Out. On the designated night, their husbands care for the children, and the women go to a restaurant for dinner or have coffee at Barnes & Noble. Sometimes, they do scrapbooking or take in a movie or window shop at the mall. After a few hours away, they come back home refreshed and ready to tackle the next day's challenges. It doesn't take a big group for a fun evening. Even if you have one other mom, you can start a Girls' Night Out and perhaps find other friends along the way who'd like to join you.

Get involved at your child's school. If your children are school age, a great way to meet other moms is to join the PTA or other parents' association and find a way to use your skills and talents to contribute. Working together with other mothers, you'll discover women with interests similar to yours. As you organize projects, carnivals, or events, you'll be working toward a common goal, which will also help develop friendships. And getting to know the mothers of your children's classmates is a great benefit, especially as your children grow into the middle and high school grades.

> Two are better than one, because they have a good return for their work: If one falls down, his friend can help him up.
> —ECCLESIASTES 4:9-10

Have a neighborhood block party. Like Elaine, my neighbor who had the Christmas brunch, you could be the person who helps moms in your neighborhood connect. Have a Christmas block party or a summer ice cream social. Send out computer-generated or handmade invitations that your kids help make, plan to serve simple snacks, and ask others who are willing to bring treats. Your party might just be the answer to somebody's prayer! Making and cultivating friendships is always a two-way street. When you bring encouragement and support to another mom's life, you will be blessed beyond measure in return.

QUESTION FOR REFLECTION

How could you be a better friend today by making a phone call, sending a note of encouragement, or inviting someone to a simple lunch at your home?

12

A Mom's Greatest Gift

It was back-to-school time, which for me always brought back memories of chalk dust (which I was allergic to), freshly waxed classroom floors, the smell of brand-spanking new, never-used books, and the lunchroom on the first pizza day.

I'd been out braving the crowds at the mall with my children purchasing blue jeans, lunch boxes, and school supplies. We'd also searched for the athletic shoe-of-the-moment, too, but were unsuccessful in finding a pair in Chris's size that day. Ads on TV and in magazines try to convince us that kids have got to have the latest computers and educational software to be successful in school and that they must have the latest gear to be successful in sports. So we parents do what we can to provide them.

The beginning of the school year isn't the only time we find ourselves at the mall or discount store buying things for our kids. There are birthdays and Christmas or special times when we find that darling something at BabyGap or Super Target for our child.

But the greatest gift we can give our children isn't found in a mall, the school supply aisle, or an online store. We don't have to charge it on plastic. It won't affect our bank account. It won't shrink or clutter the floor after its newness wears off. But it yields the biggest dividend of anything we can invest in.

This gift will outlive our lives! It's a mom's greatest influence and the best thing we can possibly do to bless our children's lives, no matter whether they are babies, toddlers, teens, in college, or somewhere in between: It's a mother's prayer.

> Again, I tell you that if two of you on earth agree about anything you ask for, it will be done for you by my Father in heaven. For where two or three come together in my name, there am I with them.
>
> —MATTHEW 18:19-20

If we let prayer be at the foundation or center of our mothering, it will be such a blessing. Look with me at what prayer can do in the life of a mother:

Through prayer comes wisdom. According to James 1, if you ask God for wisdom, He will never to turn you away but will always supply the wisdom you need if you will but ask.

And if you call to God first, as Jeremiah 33:3 says, instead of asking everyone else for their opinions, the Lord will show you things you truly need to know but would never discover without His revealing them. When you have problems, He will show you what is your part (and dad's, if he's involved), what is your child's part, and what is His part. That way, you won't try to do everyone else's part or be the Holy Spirit and, thus, get in the Lord's way! If you pray for your children and give God your worries, your energy and joy won't be sapped by anxiety. And if your marriage is centered on prayer, the unity candle will continue to burn, and there will be more intimacy and strength in your relationship.

Prayer is the greatest influence on the hearts of your children and their spiritual growth. You can take your kids to church, get them the best education, and be consistent about your family devotions, but you can't change their hearts. You can't make them love God and resist the downward slide of the culture around them. Only God through His Spirit can. But as you pray, His heart-changing power moves and strengthens your children spiritually.

"Our prayers lay the tracks on which God's power can come," said Watchman Nee, an old prayer theologian. Like a locomotive, God's power is mighty and irresistible—in fact, the mightiest force in the universe—and when you pray, it's released in the life of the person or situation needing it.

> Satan trembles when he sees the weakest saint on her knees, for he knows he has no power against our prayers.
>
> —FERN NICHOLS

Prayer is the greatest resource God has given to make a difference in our world, our homes, neighborhoods, and schools. It is also our greatest tool to fight evil and dissolve the enemy's schemes. When one small group of Tennessee moms met in a Moms In Touch group every week for one hour to pray for the high school their kids attended, change began to happen. First, cheating, drug and alcohol use, and other problems were brought to light. An honor and dress code were put in place. When the moms began praying that God would either convert or remove any teachers who were a wrong influence, 20 teachers left the first summer and 14 the next—without a word of complaint to the administration.

Eventually, several hundred teens were meeting before school for Bible study or praise and worship, and circles of kids were seen praying during breaks and at lunchtime. Can prayer make a difference? As 2 Corinthians 10:4 says, "The weapons we fight with are not the weapons of the world. On the contrary, they have divine power to demolish strongholds."

Whatever age your children are, let me encourage you to pray for them. Don't let the crush of activities and tasks distract you from the most important influence you can have on their lives. It's never too early or late to start! Here are some ways:

Walk, drive, and live praying. Ask yourself: What would be your heart's desire for God to do if you could speak to Him about your children? (You can!) What is your greatest concern for them? Write it on a card and pray as you walk or drive this week. You can also pray as you go through your day. Let visual cues be reminders. For example, when you pick up your kids' shoes, pray for their feet to stay on God's path, and when you prepare meals for the family, pray for God's Word to be their Bread of Life.

> By prayer you can live in God's presence with as little effort as you live on the very air you are now breathing.
>
> —MADAME GUYON

Let Scripture shape your prayers for your children. When you pray God's Word for your children, for example, *Lord, I ask that Meghan will trust in You with all her heart and not lean on her own understanding (Proverbs 3:5-6),* your prayers bear fruit because you're asking in agreement with God's stated will. And as a side benefit, you are filled with confidence and faith. The Bible is full of prayers to pray for your kids.

Join with other moms. God hears your prayers while you're rocking a feverish baby at midnight, while you're cooking or carpooling, or when you're on your knees—and those prayers make a difference. But the power multiplies when you join with other moms! One way to pray intentionally and faithfully one hour a week is with a Moms In Touch group. You can visit momsintouch.org for more information and to find or start a group in your community.

Your prayers are the greatest gift you can give your children—one that keeps on giving far beyond school days and holidays.

QUESTION FOR REFLECTION

Who prayed for you when you were growing up? Your mom, grandma, another family member, a Sunday school teacher? Take a few moments to thank God for them and the impact of their prayers on your life.

13

Great Expectations

The 11-year-old stepped up to the podium and took the microphone, beaming a huge smile as he began to deliver a dynamic keynote message to 8,000 car wash owners at their national convention in Las Vegas. His parents and friends watched and clapped, full of joy at all he had achieved.

It would be an accomplishment for any child to speak to an audience of thousands of adults and keep his cool, but especially for this boy. Brian was born with Williams Syndrome, which causes heart problems and retardation. He had other disabilities and medical challenges as well.

Although his teachers said he'd never learn to read, his mom and dad continued to have high hopes for him. They encouraged him to build on his strengths, especially his interest in car washes, which ultimately led to his learning to read. His mother, Valerie, made flash cards out of car wash words, and his vocabulary grew and grew. With perseverance and much prayer, their great expectations paid off. Brian became an avid reader and the car wash industry's number-one fan. He was invited to speak at many conventions for the car wash industry and has a dream of owning his own car wash business someday.

Just like Brian, kids who overcome obstacles and succeed have something in common: a parent who has high expectations for them and believes in them, someone who encourages them to keep on trying and shows them ways to use their God-given strengths to compensate for their weaknesses.

Children are likely to live up to what you believe of them.

—LADY BIRD JOHNSON

Yet with all the negative labels the educational system sticks on kids these days, we often lower our expectations of what they can accomplish. And that produces a downward spiral. The negative label leads to low expectations, which lead to less effort and,

Kids Who Overcame Great Odds

• She was hearing impaired but became an accomplished ballerina and Miss America.

• His teachers called him "addled," and he dropped out after only six months of formal schooling. But his mom believed in him and tutored him. When he grew up he patented 1,093 inventions, including the light bulb, motion pictures, and the phonograph.

• Illness destroyed her sight and hearing before age two, but she graduated from college, was an accomplished speaker and author, and spent her life helping the blind and deaf.

• He had a 95 percent hearing loss yet became a top-notch student and gifted athlete who made it as a pro baseball player.

Curtis Pride
Helen Keller
Thomas Edison
Heather Whitestone

thus, less learning and achievement. What we expect from kids is usually what we get!

No matter what your children's abilities or challenges, your expectations have a powerful impact on their behavior, achievement, and learning. So here are some ways to develop and communicate great expectations:

Discover what is good. No matter what their problems, handicaps, or personalities, make a list of each of your children's gifts, abilities, skills, and spiritual gifts. Include good character qualities and personality strengths. Look for the treasures within each child and ask God to show you ways to develop these gifts.

Consider your child's age and capabilities so that expectations are reasonable. Otherwise, if they are unattainable—like getting a 100 on every test or winning every soccer game—kids get discouraged.

> "For I know the plans I have for you," declares the LORD, "plans to prosper you and not to harm you, plans to give you hope and a future."
>
> —JEREMIAH 29:11
>
> (A WONDERFUL VERSE FOR YOUR CHILD TO MEMORIZE.)

Take heart if your child is struggling in a certain area. All kids' brains start out immature, and spurts in maturity occur once or twice a year (or more). When a spurt occurs, it's as if a new computer chip has entered the brain. And when that chip starts firing, there's often a growth spurt in learning. Hooray! Some math concept that didn't click six months ago begins to make sense, or your child has a new understanding of science he didn't have before.

Last, avoid writing off as failures kids who aren't "test smart" and don't make the top grades at school. Also, avoid throwing cold water on their dreams by saying, "You can't do that" when they think of a project or future goal. Hopes and dreams keep us motivated and excited about life. So keep expecting and believing the best, and communicate your high hopes with encouraging words. That's because what makes the difference for a child who has big challenges yet overcomes them is someone who keeps believing in him and doesn't give up on him even if things are rough.

A child's talents are seeds that will grow only when they are planted, watered, and allowed time to blossom.

—MILES MCPHERSON

QUESTION FOR REFLECTION

What do you expect from your child in different areas such as homework, reading, and chores? Ask God to give you His expectations for her, and make the commitment to pray, equip, and encourage until the fulfillment comes.

14

Go Fly a Kite

My little boys peered through the icy window, fascinated by the snowflakes falling from the sky. Having just moved to Tulsa, Oklahoma, from central Texas, where it snowed only once every five years if you were lucky, they were awed by the first snowstorm of the season.

"Mommy, look! It's snowing! Let's go out and play!" Justin said.

"Later, honey," I said as I rushed past to put the laundry away.

"You gotta see the icicles on the roof!" he cried. When I saw their expressions fade into disappointment at my lack of excitement about their discovery, I sat down beside them and gazed at the dancing snowflakes outside. And when dad got home with warm snow boots, we all four went out and made a snowman.

Have you ever responded with "later" to one of your kids' discoveries? Has your sense of wonder faded between the pages of your Day-Timer or been replaced by practicality, busyness, and preoccupation with work and worry?

I admit it: Mine did. As I got busier with responsibilities like supervising homework, helping in my husband's business, juggling housework, and keeping up with writing deadlines, I started missing many of the magical, miraculous things God had put in my line of vision. I was so task-oriented I forgot how to play. I wanted to share in my kids' joy and sense of discovery, but there was so much to do!

Finally, frustrated, I asked the Lord, *Help. Any suggestions?*

He seemed to say, *Go fly a kite.*

I don't even own a kite and besides, that seems so impractical, I thought.

That's just the point, He answered.

So I purchased a kite for our next family time at the park. Holmes is great at deciphering directions, so with all of us working together, we got it up. After a few minutes of holding the string, my kids ran off to swing and slide, leaving me holding the kite.

> I will be glad and rejoice in you; I will sing praise to your name, O Most High.
>
> —PSALM 9:2

As the big red, yellow, and black kite caught the wind and flew higher and higher, my spirit soared too. After that afternoon, I was hooked on kites. There are plenty of windy days in Oklahoma, so kite-flying opportunities abounded. I kept the kite in the trunk and brought it out whenever we walked around a local lake or, on rare occasions, we got to travel to the beach. Looking up, I relished God's handiwork—the birds flying overhead, the big Oklahoma blue sky, or a puffy cascade of clouds—instead of focusing on my own earthly problems. It stirred my sense of wonder and refreshed my spirit. As I slowed down a bit, I found my heart drawn upward, toward God.

Flying a kite is just a metaphor for doing something for no

reason at all except that it's fun. Today I'm at the beach, still flying a kite after all these years, even though the kids have sprouted wings and flown away to their own homes. It's a little kite—purple, turquoise, and green striped. But while flying it, I've seen some spectacular clouds and enjoyed the cool breeze off the water. Some children just came over, wanting to hold the string. I'll take it home so my four-year-old granddaughter, Caitlin, can have fun flying it.

If, like me, you've been in your office or laundry room too much, let me encourage you...go fly a kite.

You see, I think God wants us to be the kind of moms who don't take little things like cool breezes, sunrises, hummingbirds, new babies, and good health for granted. He wants us to be filled with awe and gratefulness at His amazing grace. When we are, our hearts will be refreshed and inevitably splash some joy on those around us.

> Deep inside we know the truth: The lights of love and relationship don't snap on like a floodlight at the flip of a magic switch. They twinkle on—one at a time—like stars, like the fireflies glowing from the unexpected corners of a still summer night.
>
> —DEENA LEE WILSON

If kite-flying isn't your cup of tea (or the weather's not permitting), here are some other ways to stir up your wonder:

Let's blow bubbles. Mix liquid dishwashing soap and one teaspoon of glycerine. Then have a bubble-blowing blast with your children using a straw, a colander, plastic six-pack cola rings, and other utensils.

Create a backyard wildlife habitat. Put a bird feeder and birdbath in your backyard or on the balcony. Let your child help plant flowers that attract butterflies. Then get a book to identify the feathered friends that visit your sanctuary.

Tell the temperature cricket-style. Just count a cricket's chirps for 15 seconds, then add 40 to that number to find out the temperature. (It's good math practice, too). Your kids will think you are very clever.

> Sometimes...
> let's just blow bubbles,
> for no good reason,
> let's just blow bubbles.
> Laugh a little, watch them disappear,
> Smile and touch the rainbow colors.
>
> —RUTH REARDON

Watch a sunset. Sit on a big quilt in the yard with your kids and watch the sky at sunset—how remarkable it is that every few minutes the colors of the sky change as blue melts into purple and the sky becomes darker and darker. Have hot chocolate or cider after you come in, and talk about what you saw.

Catch a falling star. Get a constellation map for the current season from a local planetarium. Choose a clear, moonless night. Locate the North Star, Big Dipper, and Orion. Binoculars or a telescope are nice but not necessary. You might see a surprise or two, like a shooting star or meteor shower, or maybe one of the bright planets like Venus.

QUESTION FOR REFLECTION

What is it that makes your spirit soar? You might find it outdoors, in an art museum, at a symphony concert, on a trip to a botanical garden, or perhaps right in your own backyard.

15

Trust Your Heart

The lights in the main room of the church dimmed. We were all in rapt attention as the video began. Along with all the other parents in our congregation, my husband and I had been urged to attend the showing of this parenting video and to read the accompanying book, which presented a system guaranteed to produce well-behaved, obedient, godly children.

As we watched, the formula was clearly spelled out through examples and instructions: If your child doesn't obey you the first time, spank him. Strive for unquestioned obedience. Don't allow your kids to say "no." If they do something wrong, assume it's rebellion or misbehavior and punish swiftly (with corporal punishment, spanking being the most recommended consequence). If you follow this formula consistently, the result will be well-trained children.

During the presentation, Bible verses were flashed on the screen, assuring all those watching that this was the biblical way of raising children. Following the video, the pastor encouraged each family to follow the prescribed parenting practices just as he and the other church leaders were already doing.

As Holmes and I drove home that night, it was all quiet on

the western front...or at least in our car. The program was very convincing, but when we began to talk and pray about what we'd seen, both Holmes and I sensed red flags about this parenting system. The harshness, the rigidity, the ignoring of children's emotional needs were just a few of our concerns.

So although we watched the presentation with the rest of the parents, we didn't embrace its principles. However, seeing it did stir up some good dialogue and help us realize we already had a good balance of love and discipline (and unity as a couple), and we didn't feel that replacing our parenting style to jump on this particular trend would be God's best for our family. We trusted our hearts and how God had been guiding us as parents.

It was hard when I was criticized by other moms, like the one who said one afternoon after we'd been together, "You know, you just are too merciful with your children. You err on the side of compassion when you should be tougher like they taught in the video." Actually, I think the Bible recommends mercy over judgment, but at the time, her criticism hurt.

> Train a child in the way he should go [and in keeping with his individual gift or bent], and when he is old he will not turn from it.
>
> —PROVERBS 22:6

As we look back over the years and those families who did go with the heavy-handed, forced compliance method, we saw a high percentage of open and, in some cases, tragic rebellion among their teenagers. Many of these Christian kids grew to resent their parents instead of having healthy relationships with them. And as soon as they could drive, they were out of there—getting as far away from their parents' values and beliefs as they could.

Holmes and I weren't smarter or better parents, but perhaps we've seen good fruit borne because we listened to God's guidance for our family and we parented our children together. It also helped that I'd read some excellent resources on child development and parenting from which I learned that unconditional love is the foundation needed in a child's life, and that children whose emotional tanks have been filled up respond more positively to correction.

> Fathers [mothers], do not embitter your children, or they will become discouraged.
>
> —COLOSSIANS 3:21

What can you do when everyone seems to be going to a certain parenting class or following the same book or formula for raising the ideal Christian kids? Here are a few suggestions:

Don't set your focus on accomplishing short-term, perfect-acting kids at the expense of growing emotionally healthy young people. And don't major on behavior control as the primary way to relate to your child. Meeting your children's emotional needs should be a priority in all your parenting, not controlling them primarily with punishment.[5]

Read, pray, develop your plan, and be united. Jehoshaphat's prayer in 2 Chronicles 20:12, "Lord, I don't know what to do, [for this child, in this particular situation] but my eyes are on you," is always a great prayer for parents. I encourage you to do more praying than reacting.

Read the Bible, along with sound resources on child development, as a foundation for life and parenting. It will help you know what to expect from your children at each age and help you distinguish childish irresponsibility from outright defiance or intentional misbehavior.

Don't just take one resource and latch on to it as a formula. Read widely enough to know what you believe is best for your family. If you have some discipline challenges or are looking for help, read books like *Boundaries for Kids* (Cloud and Townsend), *The New Dare to Discipline* (Dobson), *Touchpoints* (Brazelton), and *Parenting with Love & Logic* (Fay and Cline).

Think of a book or resource as providing overall principles and giving you ideas, not as some "Bible" for parenting that you must follow to the letter of the law. For example, if the current healthy sleep book says that the *only* good sleep for babies is in their cribs and anything else is "junk sleep," and you follow such a system too rigidly, you may miss out on some wonderful chances to snuggle with your baby in your bed (and no, your baby won't refuse to sleep in his crib forevermore). Remember, opinions vary widely between experts on many matters of child-rearing: Some say that if you don't give your baby a bottle between 3-8 weeks when you're breastfeeding, they'll never take one; other camps say don't start the bottle too early because it will cause nipple confusion. Let me encourage you to avoid extremes and not become a slave to any one system.

> An easily controlled child is set up for a lot of problems in life. He doesn't have the strength to say no, so when he gets to preadolescence, he doesn't have much defense. In effect, by forcing our control on a kid, we are increasing the probability that the jaws of the peer group will rip that kid apart.
> —KEVIN LEMAN

Most of all, ask for and listen to God's direction for each of your children, and trust your heart as you and your spouse sense unity on parenting issues. And remember, you are the mom God picked out of all the potential mothers in the world to love, nurture, and raise your precious child.

Recognize the diverse makeup of each of your kids. "Diverse children have their different natures," said Anne Bradstreet, a colonial American mother and poet. "Some are like flesh which nothing but salt will keep from putrefaction, some like tender fruits that are best preserved with sugar. Those parents are wise that can fit their nurture according to their children's natures." I encourage you to think about the unique discipline dilemmas you face with each of your children. One discipline doesn't fit all. Which child needs a sensitive, gentle approach (sugar)? Which child responds to verbal correction? Which one needs firmer discipline (salt)? Pray for the discernment to know which is best for each one, and consider the most appropriate discipline for a particular child and behavior problem.

Don't assume that one parenting system is right for all families and all children just because it has a Christian label or the author says it's God's way. How wonderful that God promises us His wisdom if we ask for it—wisdom to prepare our kids for life and to be the kind of moms and dads they need in order to become all He created them to be!

QUESTION FOR REFLECTION

Think about each of your children. What kind of discipline do they respond to: requests, commands, punishment (spanking or time out), logical consequences? What does each of them need?

16

Gratitude Is a Memory of the Heart

One day Heather, one of the moms at the pediatric cancer clinic where I volunteer, said, "Let's start a list of things we're grateful for. We can all brainstorm what we're thankful for. Cheri, you can write it on big pieces of paper on the wall, and the kids can illustrate it. Other children can add to the list when they come to the clinic, and it'll remind us all about things to give thanks for."

Five-year-old Hunter immediately said, "Fast yellow-and-gray cars. That's what I'm thankful for."

It is good to praise the LORD . . .

—PSALM 92:1

"Faith and the strength it gives me," Heather said.

"God," one of the kids called out.

"Heart-shaped balloons. Blood and marrow donors. My purple tennis shoes," said other children.

"Mom!" Cody yelled.

"Volunteers who take time to provide a little sunshine for our kids. For waking up each morning. My child's smile," parents added.

Squishy bugs, double rainbows, puddles to jump in after the rain, the new hair I have growing in, riding the tractor with Daddy...the list went on and on.

Gratitude *does* warm and encourage the soul. In fact, psychologists proclaim the enormous benefits of expressing thanks. These moms whose children were having painful cancer treatments, facing uncertainty and more than their share of troubles, could have focused on the negative and grown more depressed. But as their thankful list grew and grew, it shifted their minds from negative thoughts to more healthy ones, helped put problems in perspective, and gave them hope. The same is true in our lives. And when we express that thanks to God and someone else, it's a double blessing.

> If gratitude is due from children to their earthly parent, how much more is the gratitude of the great family of men to our Father in heaven.
>
> —HOSEA BALLOU

Here are some ways to stir up gratitude in your family:

Model a grateful attitude. Give thanks openly for the things your spouse does that you normally take for granted. Your kids will be influenced by your example. Research shows that the biggest impact on kids' values is the relationship they observe between their mom and dad. Also, as you express appreciation for who your children are and the positive things they do, it helps them see how to affirm people (and boosts their sense of self-worth at the same time).

Make a "Blessing Basket." Place a basket in the middle of the dinner table and encourage each family member to write their favorite blessings of the day on index cards or sticky notes. Then every few days, read the notes aloud to remind everyone of the many good things that happen in our lives every day (and don't forget to thank God for them too).

The most important prayer in the world is just two words long: "Thank you."

—Meister Eckhart

Play "Alphabet Thanks." When you carpool to school or activities, or when you're around the dinner table, have one child name something she's grateful for that begins with the letter *A*. Move on to *B, C,* and so on through the alphabet.

Start a new tradition. Whenever you shop for birthday or Christmas gifts, pick out small boxes of thank-you notes for your children. Then designate a time for them to sit down and write a short note to each person who gave them a gift. If your kids are too young to write, have them dictate their thank-you notes to you, and let them illustrate the notes with original pictures.

By leaving a trail of gratitude in your family's life, a thankful spirit will warm your hearts, not for just one day in November but throughout the year.

QUESTION FOR REFLECTION

Think back across the years. Can you remember a teacher, mentor, or relative who positively impacted your life? Perhaps a Sunday school teacher, a pastor, or music teacher? Have you ever told that person what a difference they made in your life? List a few people who come to mind, then send a note of appreciation to one of them.

17

Create a Quilt
of Memories

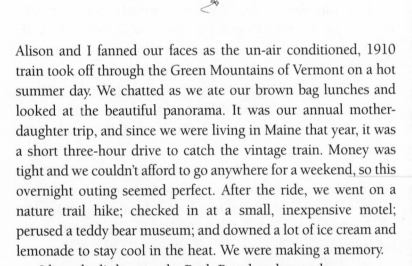

Alison and I fanned our faces as the un-air conditioned, 1910 train took off through the Green Mountains of Vermont on a hot summer day. We chatted as we ate our brown bag lunches and looked at the beautiful panorama. It was our annual mother-daughter trip, and since we were living in Maine that year, it was a short three-hour drive to catch the vintage train. Money was tight and we couldn't afford to go anywhere for a weekend, so this overnight outing seemed perfect. After the ride, we went on a nature trail hike; checked in at a small, inexpensive motel; perused a teddy bear museum; and downed a lot of ice cream and lemonade to stay cool in the heat. We were making a memory.

I love the little poem by Ruth Reardon that reads…

Create a quilt of memories to keep me warm.

An inner warmth that comes from light of happy times.

Weave in the threads of holidays, of friends, and families…

Delights of seashore, fields, of city parks.

The simplest happenings traced out in love

Become a pattern, for my quilt of memories.

As moms, we have the wonderful privilege of planting seeds and building memories in our children's lives. Seeds and memories of caring for them when they're sick; sharing their excitement when they bring home awards and good report cards; listening to their side when they get into trouble at school or are going through a difficult, lonely time. Seeds and memories of hugs and hope and forgiveness and happy times together flying kites or riding bikes or reading stories.

> There is a time for everything, and a season for every activity under heaven.
>
> —ECCLESIASTES 3:1

Consciously or not, we are always making memories for our children. We can aim for making a quilt of memories that, little by little, creates in our children a sense of belonging, of what it means to be a family, of security and continuity in life. Then

Family Memory Makers

- Pajama Day: Slow your family's hectic pace by taking a day just to chill. Declare "Pajama Day" and get out big pillows and sleeping bags. Snuggle, read stories, play games, and watch a movie.
- Family Watercolor Night: Have each person paint his favorite vacation spot or place the family has been to.
- Create a Book: Help your kids make a book about their life. Pick some photos, and have them write about what's happening in each one. (For little ones, you'll need to write as they dictate.) Include the child's birth date, current handprint and footprint, drawings of themselves and the family, and life story. It makes a wonderful keepsake.

when they become parents, they will draw from that reservoir of memories, some tucked away so far they didn't remember they were there, to love and care for their children.

Building memories with our Alison was important to me, partly because she's the only daughter. Also, losing my parents early in life has always reminded me that life is short, and I wanted to make time for just being together. (Don't get me wrong. I built memories with our two sons also, but in this chapter I want to share specifically about mother-daughter memories.)

> What is a family meant to be? Among other things, I personally have always felt it is meant to be a museum of memories—collections of carefully preserved memories and a realization that day-by-day memories are being chosen for our museum.... what is done today will be tomorrow's memory.
>
> —EDITH SCHAEFFER

Here are some ways I built our relationship and made memories with Alison, even during her prickly teenage years:

Tuning in. As a mom, I was a fixer by nature who wanted everyone to be happy. I had to work at tuning in to Alison when she said things like "I had a horrible day. I have so much homework I'll never get it done, and the teachers keep piling it on. They make me so mad!" I found that responding, "You must be really frustrated with all that work" instead of "If you just planned your time better, you'd be okay" helped our communication stay open.

Taking mother-daughter trips or outings. Just like the train trip we went on when Alison was 11, each year we planned some kind of getaway. Another year we traveled to a nearby city for an overnight stay, went ice skating then to a movie, listened to the Focus on the Family *Preparing for Adolescence* tapes, and talked about growing up. Sometimes it was a short, in-town outing like attending the summer musical at the live theater. When she was 12, I happened to be near Florida on a business trip, so Ali saved her baby-sitting money for tickets to Disney World. We stayed with a family we knew and took three days to explore the magical world of Disney together.

> Be a mother. It's a rewarding thing. Mothers and Christmas are the two best things in the world…. But my mother is the best gift I ever got.
>
> —MARIE, AGE 9

Seizing serendipity moments. Making memories at Christmas or other special times is wonderful. But some of the best memories are made in those serendipity moments that just happen— like when your daughter comes in after lights out and curls up beside you, or when you take time out from running errands for a smoothie and a chat, or when you take a walk together. It's in these short, unexpected times that dreams and hopes and secrets are shared, things are laughed about, or you get a little glimpse of how God is working.

We weathered her adolescent years and Alison, now 26, is married with a baby of her own and another on the way. She and I still love to meet for breakfast or coffee, and we continue to build memories. As her little one, Noah, has come into the family, our quilt of memories is expanding and growing…simple happenings traced in love.

QUESTION FOR REFLECTION
What's your favorite memory from your childhood? What's your favorite memory with your daughter or son?

18

Words That Work

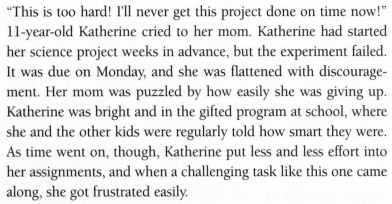

"This is too hard! I'll never get this project done on time now!" 11-year-old Katherine cried to her mom. Katherine had started her science project weeks in advance, but the experiment failed. It was due on Monday, and she was flattened with discouragement. Her mom was puzzled by how easily she was giving up. Katherine was bright and in the gifted program at school, where she and the other kids were regularly told how smart they were. As time went on, though, Katherine put less and less effort into her assignments, and when a challenging task like this one came along, she got frustrated easily.

"I know you're upset, but you'll just need to focus your efforts on finding a new experiment, following the instructions, and doing the work." With only three days left, Katherine picked a project that demonstrated the concept of the center of gravity and, with her mom's help, began working on the display. With praise for each part of the work Katherine completed, Karen saw her daughter's efforts grow. She even stuck with the boring part of writing out the scientific process and got the whole thing done on time.

Even better, Katherine ended up winning first place. Her

mom let her know that it was her effort that had made the difference.

> Too often parents get extremely caught up in the grades,
> and then they say to their child, "Why doesn't this motivate
> you?" What is motivating is the whole process of learning and
> the excitement and challenge of it.
>
> —DR. DAVID ELKIND

We all know that encouraging our kids and telling them what
a good job they are doing on schoolwork or sports is important,
but there's very interesting research showing that we often praise
our kids in a way that backfires. Let me explain.

A Columbia University research project studied over 400 fifth
graders to discover what worked best with a series of math tests:
praising kids for intelligence ("Wow, that's a high score! You are
really smart at this.") or effort ("You got ten right. You must have
worked really hard to get that high score!").

Guess which kids were boosted in their motivation? Which
kind of praise worked better?

The effort-praised kids—not the students praised for being
smart—did the best, not only on the first test but also on future
ones. Here's how it worked: When children were praised for how
much effort they'd put into preparing for the test, they studied
more for the next test. When they encountered tough problems,
they thought it meant they needed to try harder. As a result, their
scores went up, and they were less likely to lie about their marks
or cheat.

However, the kids praised for their intelligence began to
avoid risks to keep looking smart. In subsequent tests, they
showed a drop in effort and interest in the subject and were more

apt to lie about their scores or cheat to get a high grade. When they encountered harder problems and didn't do well, they thought, *I'm not good at this*, and they stopped trying. Because they gave less effort, these students made lower scores on each subsequent test.

> Do not let any unwholesome talk come out of your mouths, but only what is helpful for building others up according to their needs, that it may benefit those who listen.
>
> —EPHESIANS 4:29

What can you do to praise and encourage your kids in a way that helps them and fuels their motivation?

- Let them know that effort is a key ingredient in all pursuits in life.
- Focus on the work, effort, and time they are putting into schoolwork, sports, or other pursuits.
- Let them know you value the content of what they are learning, not just the grades or report cards.
- Focus on what they are doing well, not what they are lacking. Affirm whatever progress is made, even if it is small!
- When your child brings home a great score, say something like "Terrific! I'm proud of you—you worked hard and put lots of effort into learning the material."
- When your child has trouble with homework, respond with "Let's look at the problem, break it down, and work step by step to figure it out." Refocusing on the task and formulating a strategy encourages effort and steers him away from negative conclusions like "I'm just not good at math!"

As you use words that work, you'll find the effort-boosting

effects are long-lasting and will help your children face challenges in the future, whether in school, sports, or life.

QUESTION FOR REFLECTION

What is one way your words could encourage your child in a current school subject or learning experience?

A good mother is somebody who doesn't yell at you for getting a bad grade. She understands, because maybe she got a bad one sometime too.

—ROBERTA, AGE 8

19

Connecting with Your Kids on Their Turf

One morning I sat at the Classen Grill, a local restaurant, with our 26-year-old son, Chris, having breakfast to celebrate his upcoming birthday. He was going to be out of town with his wife, Maggie, on his actual birthday, so it was our chance to chat and celebrate at his favorite breakfast place. Chris is our quietest child and, at that time, was a third-year medical student who had a grueling hospital schedule.

Having "special time" is something we started when Chris was very young, and I realized this sports lover who was growing taller every day (he's now 6' 3") wasn't going to sit down to visit or shop at the mall with me—unless we were looking for Nike Air Jordans for him.

I discovered that the best way to connect with Chris was to get on his turf—in other words, do what he liked and enjoyed. So, many afternoons after school, I started asking him when he came in the door, "You want to shoot some hoops?" or "Chris, want to play Ping-Pong or throw the baseball?" and out in the yard we'd go. There, he'd slowly begin to open up and tell me what was going on at school or on the basketball team, or he'd talk about a friend or a test coming up. I'd hear what he was thinking and certainly much more than I'd ever have known if we hadn't gotten on his turf.

"My 12-year-old just isn't talking to me anymore. He used to tell me everything, and now he just clams up," a mom told me recently. I shared with her that kids' emotions and thoughts are much like oatmeal. If you heat up a pot of oatmeal, as it gets hotter, the bubbles come to the surface. Similarly, as children or teens get "heated up" through activities they enjoy, their emotions and thoughts bubble up to the surface, and they begin to talk about them. You begin to connect. You hear what's troubling them and what they're excited about.

So I asked her, "What's your son's turf?" It turned out to be golf, so occasionally, she drove the cart for him when he played after school, and she even went to the driving range with him. For another kid it might be skateboarding (it would be really hard for me to get on that kind of turf!) or kicking the soccer ball, jogging, cooking, or doing crafts. It doesn't have to take long or cost much. Just find out what the turf is and begin doing it together, and the lines of communication will often open up.

Live a life of love.

—EPHESIANS 5:2

Here are two ways to start this relationship-building strategy with your kids:

Be accessible. Accessibility means being easy to approach, being open and warm, not distant. That means being available to give "focused attention," a combination of eye contact, physical contact, and shared activity. As you fill your children's emotional tanks in this way, they'll begin to let you know what they're interested in, what they're feeling, what's bothering them or making them happy. They will feel loved for who they are, not just for what they do.

Be flexible. Your children's turf will likely change as they grow older. When our daughter was in elementary school, she'd always take me up on a bike ride, but as a teenager, she liked to spend time with me window-shopping at the mall and stopping for a soda. Now she likes to meet at Starbucks for an espresso. When our son Justin was young, getting on his turf meant playing LEGOs and, later, tennis with him. But in college, he asked me to meet him at his university campus to hear a lecture on the creation/evolution controversy presented by a brilliant attorney.

> Parents of teens and parents of babies have something in common. They spend a great deal of time trying to get their kids to talk.
>
> —PAUL SWET

Remember, don't spend time on your child's turf just as a reward for performance or as a duty, but as a way to share and talk about something together or as a way to open up conversation.

A renowned family and child psychologist in our city believed in focused attention so much that if parents came into his office seeking help for a child's behavior problem, he asked them to spend 30 minutes each day for a month doing something with the child that he liked and enjoyed. If the behavior problem remained after a month of consistent "filling of the emotional tank," he offered his counseling services to that family free of charge (instead of $100 an hour). This kind of parent-child time worked so well that when mom and dad really followed through on daily emotional-tank filling, they rarely needed his counseling to "fix" their child!

QUESTION FOR REFLECTION

What's your child's turf? Find out what he most enjoys doing or is most interested in and do it together.

20

You've Been on My Mind

I was racing through the Dallas/Ft. Worth airport on the way to my gate when a rack of greeting cards caught my eye. Although I was late and 10 gates away, I decided to stop and buy a card for my husband, Holmes. A Mary Engelbreit design that read "You've been on my mind" seemed perfect.

> In a child's lunch box, a mother's thoughts.
>
> —JAPANESE PROVERB

A few moments later, when I was crammed into the American Airlines shuttle bus with a bunch of other weary travelers, one of the pilots in front of me took his hat off to wipe his brow. (There was lots of brow-wiping because it was about 90 degrees inside the bus.) There, taped inside the pilot's hat, was a full-color photo of his wife and two sons.

The pilot gazed at the picture wistfully, as if he were thinking how much he'd like to be with them right then instead of on his way to another three-day flight schedule. Then he put his hat back on. I don't know how many planes this man had to fly before returning home, but for the rest of the trip, his family would be sitting right on his head. They might be out of sight but not out of mind!

I couldn't help thinking that when this pilot-dad arrives home and his kids and wife see his hat, they must feel loved, knowing *He's been thinking about me—I've been on his mind.*

Do your kids and husband know they're on your mind? Life goes so fast for most of us, and it's easy for your loved ones to feel lost in the busyness of your life, your urgent "To Do" list, or your travel schedule.

> Do you love me
> Or do you not?
> You told me once
> But I forgot.
>
> —ANONYMOUS

Here are some simple ways to let them know they've been on your mind whether you're at home or away:

Plant a picture. Put your family's photo where you'll see it (and they'll be able to sneak a peek sometimes too), for example, inside the visor of your car if you spend a lot of time driving, or by your computer or workstation. I have a family photo inside my mouse pad, and pictures of my grandchildren are the screen saver on my computer, constantly reminding me of what and who are most important in my life.

Trace a hand. Often our kids don't know we're praying for them. Get some card stock in several different colors, and trace your children's hands. Cut out the hands, write a child's name and a verse you're praying for them on each hand, then put the paper hands in your Bible or prayer journal. When the kids ask you what they're for, you can share that you want to be able to put your hand on their handprint when you're praying for them every day.

> Therefore encourage one another and build each other up, just as in fact you are doing.
>
> —1 THESSALONIANS 5:11

Leave a lunch box love note. When kids or grown-ups find a note in an unexpected place that says, "I love you" or "I'm missing you," it warms the heart and fills their love tank. Greeting cards for no special reason are great, but so are yellow sticky notes on the mirror that say, "Have a wonderful day. Love, Mom." Even preschoolers who can't read will decode the message in their lunch box by finding somebody to read it to them. (It's also a great motivator for learning to read.) You can also tuck little notes inside a suitcase packed for camp or a business trip, or on their pillows when you are out for the evening.

QUESTION FOR REFLECTION

When was the last time you told your husband (or child) you love him in a way that matches his love language? Would he receive your love best if you said it with physical affection, like a hug or sitting close to him during a football game on TV? Is he a word person who likes to read words of admiration in a card? Is he a giver who'd love to receive a thoughtful gift from you?

21

Letting Go

I remember the warm summer afternoon I was sitting in the white wooden porch swing and our 15-year-old son, Justin, shirtless in his khaki shorts, was sitting next to me. My arm around him, I patted his tanned shoulder as he told me about his plans to rock climb, rappel, and hike at the Young Life camp he was leaving for the next day. And then my hand made a startling discovery—his muscles had changed.

Could this be the same arm that once belonged to a skinny little boy? I wondered. His muscles were denser, causing me to take notice of what had escaped me before: My firstborn son was rapidly changing from a boy to a man. He was taller, peach fuzz had become prickles demanding an every-other-day shave, and he was asking for the car keys.

As we rocked back and forth in the swing, I can't honestly say this realization brought a smile of delight to my face. Instead, a tear began to form from somewhere deep inside and made its way down my cheek as I recalled other days of rocking—in the antique yellow rocker I'd found for $10, restored, and stitched a needlepoint cushion for. I remembered how the chair squeaked as I daily grew larger with child and nursed first one, then another, and another baby. Memories came flooding back of rocking them to sleep when they were sick or fretful, of rocking and reading *Goodnight Moon* and *Little Visits with God*.

Only a few years later our next son, Christopher, and I sat in the porch swing—on a different deck and in a different season. The leaves on the grapevine above us had fallen to the ground. The paint on the swing had chipped. Our discussion turned to the colleges he wanted to visit before Christmas. I thought, *How I'll miss hearing his car stereo blare as he pulls into the driveway after school and seeing his long 6' 3" frame stretched out in front of an ESPN sports event in our family room. How will we make it through the week without cheering his volleyball, basketball, and baseball games after school?*

And then it seemed like we'd only turned around a few times before our youngest child and only daughter, Alison, was walking across the stage in a shiny red cap and gown, face glowing and full of hope…and then we were putting her on a plane as she left for a mission trip across the ocean.

> For it is God who is at work [in your children], both to will and to work for His good pleasure.
>
> —PHILIPPIANS 2:13, NASB

I think letting go is perhaps the hardest work of motherhood, and that's why we moms struggle with it. Letting go starts way before your child officially leaves the nest. You may have run into it the first day your daughter picked up her shiny lunch box and got on the huge yellow bus, heading off to school. Or in the emergency room or when she went to summer camp. Or you may have avoided it until the day your son loaded his stuff into his car, flashed you a grin that cost $5,000 in orthodontist bills, and drove off to college. Letting go happens in stages and also in defining moments. But as moms, all of us face it.

In *Ragman and Other Cries of Faith,* Walter Wangerin says the pain of childbearing is not one and once. "It's twofold and it comes twice; and I am astonished by the love revealed in such a miracle." First, there's making space in our body for our baby. Then we empty the space at the end of carrying our infant for nine months and deliver her "whole and squalling into existence." But this labor isn't enough. As mothers, we are asked to do it all over again! We sacrifice many things to give our child space to grow, Wangerin says: our schedule, our time, our sleep, perhaps our career, our beauty. But at the same time we experience amazing spurts of joy as we see our child begin to walk, talk, build, learn.

But then at the child's maturity, comes the "second suffering," when we must birth our child not out of our body but out of our house and into the world as an independent being. As Wangerin says...

It doesn't matter how much she has invested in raising him. By stages, now, she labors to let him go. By degrees she loosens the reins, knowing full well the danger to which she sends her child, yet fearing the greater danger of clinging to him forever. And now her hurt is the hurt that *he* will encounter on his own. (Will he survive in a careless existence, and thrive?) And beside that, her hurt is loneliness. To be, he must first be *gone.*

This is childbearing at its most laborious.

Since this letting go is inevitable, and our kids will grow up and leave home someday, what can we do to prepare for this time?

Develop rather than control. Instead of trying to control your children from the cradle to beyond college, making them perform and go the way you want, think about your role as a nurturer, developer, and coach, one who provides the "roots," or support, for growth, development, and progress but is willing to change with the seasons of each child's life. Provide a loving foundation of values and family guidelines for living, but give choices appropriate for your children's ages. Encourage them to think instead of dictating what they are to think, recognize and develop each child's gifts and uniqueness instead of trying to form them into a version of yourself, and encourage responsibility and independence instead of dependence upon on you.

> For each one of us there is a special gift, the way in which we may best serve and please the Lord whose love is so overflowing.
>
> —MADELEINE L'ENGLE

Prepare your own heart and life. Find a little space of your own—the sun porch, comfy chair in your bedroom, or a bench under a tree—and take time out to be still and nourish your own soul. Let God quiet your heart with His love, and thank Him that He is and will always be with you. When you take little breaks with the Lord, you can recharge spiritually and feel refreshed.

Develop other relationships. Avoid depending on your children for your only friendship and fellowship needs. You need girlfriends! It's also important to cultivate your marriage and not be so totally absorbed in your kids' lives that your husband's needs are ignored. You don't want to wake up when the children are gone and say to your husband, "Who are you?" because you've gotten so out of touch.

Nurture and discover the gifts God has given you. When my

children were little, I wrote poems on envelopes and the back of grocery lists. Later, I jotted them in journals, and I attended a freelance writing course at the library and a writers conference. Finally, I sent out a few stories to Christian magazines. By the time the kids were in middle and high school, I was writing from my home computer on a part-time and later, full-time basis while they were in school. Whatever gifts the Lord has given you, begin to develop them. Keep a journal. Write down dreams you have for the future and how God may be directing you.

> Kids don't stay with you if you do it right. It's one job where, the better you are, the more surely you won't be needed in the long run.
>
> —Barbara Kingsolver

As you pray for your children, release them to God. Cheryl, a mother of three grown sons, learned the wisdom of releasing them daily to the Lord as her boys grew. She prayed often, *Lord, I don't know what it's going to take to conform them to the image of Christ, but I release them into Your hands. Work within them to do Your will and purpose. These are my dreams for them, but I give these to You as well.* She was committed to love her sons and bless them, but she recognized it was God who changed and molded their hearts. By releasing her sons in prayer, she stopped wringing her hands and stressing out when one of them took a U-turn.

At some time in your children's lives, you must do what Hannah did—entrust your precious kids to God. Otherwise, you will smother, cling, try to control, and resist their efforts to become independent. When you put their hands in God's loving hands, you don't abdicate your responsibilities for teaching or nurturing them. You live with a sense that your children aren't really yours but on loan from God and that you're to care for them but not control them. And you become freer to trust God to work in their lives for their good and His glory.

QUESTION FOR REFLECTION

What aspect of your son's or daughter's life do you need to entrust to God today? What thing or desire that you're attached to needs to be released so you'll feel lighter or more content?

From the moment we awake until we fall asleep, we must commend our loved ones wholly and unreservedly to God and leave them in his hands, transforming our anxiety then into prayers on their behalf.

—DIETRICH BONHOEFFER

22

Keeping Your Kids Healthy and Fit

My granddaughter Caitlin, four, raced into the kitchen to share one of the treasures she'd found in the backyard while exploring with PaPa. Her little brother, Caleb, 19 months, toddled in and began going through the things on my lower pantry shelves and tossing them out. In a few minutes, he was out the door and riding his Little Big Wheel on the sun porch. And Noah, 9 months, crawled right after him at top speed. After keeping all three of them for a few hours, I was reminded why God gives little people to young parents!

Yet while preschoolers like my grandkids move like little Energizer bunnies, they don't stay that way. Each year from fourth grade on, children get less active and less fit, and sadly, many of them (over 30 percent) are obese. By the teen years, 63 percent of kids are sedentary and rarely move their bodies except to get up to grab more pop and chips before spending another hour on a video game.

What's the cause of this epidemic of childhood obesity? Lack of exercise and a high-fat, fast-food diet are big parts of the problem. A recent survey showed that American kids exercise less and down more fries than school-aged children in other countries. And because of the constant lure of video and computer games, TV, and movies, kids just don't move their bodies as much as they used to. In addition, many schools have eliminated physical education from the school day, and for safety reasons, most children are driven to school instead of riding their bikes or walking.

> For children, play is serious learning. Play is really the work of childhood.
>
> —FRED ROGERS

The good news is, your children can grow up healthy and fit, and the benefits are enormous. Here are a few:

- Research shows that physically fit children score higher in several areas of academic achievement. They are better able to focus and concentrate on their tasks and, thus, they enjoy school more.
- Physically fit kids have fewer chronic health problems, higher self-esteem, and are better able to meet the demands of the classroom.
- Exercise increases the body's oxygen supply, stimulates brain power, and even increases creativity!
- Physically fit kids are calmer and less anxious.

Getting fit is just a series of small steps in both eating habits and lifestyle. Here are some things you, as a mom, can do:

Be a role model. Active parents raise active kids! Take the lead and introduce your kids to a variety of physical activities and healthy eating. Remember, kids tend to do as we do, not as we say! We'll look at ways to "move your body" in the next chapter.

Don't leave out P.E. Encourage your child's school to include P.E.

as part of every day. Also, talk to the school about opening the gym on weekends and evenings so families can play together. If you're a home-school mom, incorporate exercise like jumping rope, nature walks, going to the park, or shooting baskets into your day.

An hour a day of healthy play! During after-school hours, it's crucial for kids to be active, not parked in front of the TV or computer screen (where the average American child—even preschool age—spends 25 to 30 hours a week). After active play, then they can do homework, read, or have quiet time. Avoid after-school programs that warehouse kids with VCRs and video games, and aim for at least an hour a day of healthy play and several hours of activity on the weekends.

Find out what your kids enjoy and give them opportunities to do it. Not all children are going to be soccer or baseball stars, or even enjoy competitive sports. There's also bowling, kayaking, cycle clubs, running, swimming, dance, and lots more! You could

Easy-to-Fix Foods Kids Love & Can Help Prepare

- Breakfast Sandwich: Toast a frozen waffle. Spread with peanut butter and sliced bananas.
- Fruit Smoothie: Blend fruit, fruit-flavored yogurt, low-fat milk, and ice cubes. (Add protein powder if desired.)
- Funny Face Mini Pizzas: Start with tomato sauce and veggies toasted on English muffins. Let kids use chopped olives to make eyes, zucchini for ears, cheese strips for whiskers, and a few kernels of corn for teeth.
- Adventureland Dip: Mix 2c. plain yogurt and 2T. orange or tangerine juice for a terrific dip for raw fruit slices.
- Energy Balls: Mix together $1/2$ c. nonfat dry milk, $1 1/4$ c. quick oatmeal, $1/2$ c. coconut, $1/2$ c. wheat germ, raisins, and $1/2$ c. shelled sunflower seeds. Add $1/2$ c. honey, $1/2$ c. peanut butter, and $1/3$ c. sesame seeds. Form into balls.

even build a climbing wall on your garage or playroom wall, organize a neighborhood baseball game, or take tennis lessons with your child. On rainy days, turn up the music and dance up a storm together in the living room. Walk the dog and your kids after dinner, and you'll find out lots more about their lives than if you were in front of a sitcom.

Make healthy eating fun. Take your child to the grocery store to help choose her favorite fruits and veggies, and learn to read nutrition labels. Buy fewer high-calorie, processed, low-nutrient junk foods than you did last week. Put five or six lightweight bracelets on your child's right wrist. Every time a fruit or veggie portion is eaten, move one bracelet to the other wrist. Goal: to get all the bracelets over to the other wrist by the end of the day. Encourage your kids to eat healthy to be *fit* rather than thin.

> Children are like clocks; they must be allowed to run!
> —DR. JAMES C. DOBSON

Let a finicky eater shred or chop veggies and add them to muffin mixes. Include in each meal a dish you know he'll like, and on birthdays, let each child choose the menu for his "special family dinner." When you focus on healthy food and get the whole family involved in heart-pumping, fun activities, then fitness becomes a family affair—and you'll see the benefits at home, at school, and for a lifetime.

QUESTION FOR REFLECTION

How can you provide opportunities for your children to get an hour a day of healthy play or be more physically active? What is their favorite exercise?

23

Move Your Body

Dressed in tennis shoes, old shorts, and a T-shirt, I peeked out the window shade with my 10-month-old baby, Alison, on my hip. Justin, five, and Chris, three, played G.I. Joe on the living room floor. Dinner simmered in the crock pot, the table was set, and I anxiously awaited my husband's arrival from work so I could hit the track.

Running wasn't an everyday activity of mine, but I'd been so lacking in energy trying to keep up with my three preschoolers and the household chores that many mornings I found myself asking God before my head was off the pillow, *I'm so tired, Lord. Please give me enough energy to get everything done!*

It was hard to jolt myself out of the "afternoon slump" with a cup of coffee but even harder to go for a walk with all three of the children. So I'd grown less and less active. Day after day I watched the joggers out on the track beyond my kitchen window over the sink and prayed about my fatigue. One afternoon I felt God saying, *If you want more energy, move your body.*

Finally, Holmes strolled in the door amid the whoops of the boys. I kissed him, showed him the carrot sticks and cheese-and-cracker snacks on the kitchen counter, handed him baby Alison, and then enthusiastically jogged out the door to the track behind our house.

As I made it around the track the first time, I was huffing and puffing. Passed by every runner there, I had to walk around the second and walk/run the third time. But as I did, I found the stresses of a broken washing machine, a stack of medical bills awaiting payment, and a sister I was worried about begin to melt away with the miles.

> We must move our bodies to keep them healthy.
> —HUBERTA WIERTSEMA

After doing this nightly for a while, I discovered some surprising benefits besides the increased energy I needed:

- Without dieting, I lost those last seven to eight pounds of postbaby weight. My hunger and cravings were curbed as well. (I didn't know that my brisk walk/running was speeding up my metabolism, increasing my bone density, and improving my overall health at the same time.)
- My PMS symptoms decreased. (I heard a panel of gynecologists explain recently that research has never found a more effective medication for PMS than exercise.) This was great not only for me, but the whole family.
- My mood got happier and I could handle everyday stresses better because exercise is a great mental and emotional stabilizer.
- With more energy, I had a lot more fun with my kids and my husband.

You may be thinking, *I can't take time out for me. It's too selfish and I've got too much to do.* If so, let me share an analogy with you. When I was on a plane last week, the flight attendant pulled down the yellow oxygen mask and demonstrated an important principle: Secure your mask before assisting the child seated next to you.

That principle translates for moms like this: Take care of yourself so you can take care of others—most of all, your kids and your husband. Getting enough exercise is a big component of that self-care. Mothering young children (and even elementary kids, middle schoolers, and teens) is exhausting work. You'll have more energy and stamina for the job if you regularly move your body instead of fueling yourself with candy bars, coffee, or diet colas. Here are some simple ways to begin:

> Or do you not know that your body is a temple of the Holy Spirit who is in you, whom you have from God, and that you are not your own? For you have been bought with a price: therefore glorify God in your body.
>
> —1 Corinthians 6:19-20, NASB

Start small. One thing I love about walking is you don't have to change into special clothes and work out at a gym for an hour to get fit. Aim for 20 minutes a day of brisk walking and build up to 30 minutes. In an interview with Dr. Ken Cooper, founder of The Aerobics Center in Dallas, I learned that doctors used to think you had to do aerobic exercise an hour to an hour and a half at a time to receive any benefits. But now, it's been proven that just 30 minutes a day of brisk walking (as if you are hurrying to get somewhere) will produce a good level of fitness. How can you manage that? Trade baby-sitting time with a neighbor, or get up early enough to walk before your husband goes to work.

Find a walking buddy. You're more likely to stay motivated if a friend is counting on you to show up. Susan, one of my favorite

walking partners of all time, lost 30 pounds in a year walking
with me. We kept up a pretty swift pace! Unfortunately, I didn't
lose as many pounds, but we had a great time talking and praying together as we ticked off the miles.

Walk your kids, your dog, or your husband. Besides the fact that
babies and children benefit from fresh air and are impacted positively by the role model of an active, fit mommy, your dog will
shower you with wet slobbers and be healthier, too, if you walk
him. You don't have to follow the same path every day. Walk,
don't drive, somewhere for a change. Walk with a destination
(like a local park or library) in mind. We love to walk to a nearby
breakfast café on Saturdays and stop at the farmer's market on the
way home. Mix it up to keep from getting in a rut, and vary the
time of day you walk as well. Walking with your husband is not
only good for both of you physically but also good for your marriage. Holmes and I have had some of our best heart-to-heart
talks when we were walking around the block with the kids or
our sheltie.

> Exercise is essential to get oxygen to your cells. God created
> us to be physically active. Oxygen brings life to our body…
> detoxifies our blood, strengthens our immune system,
> heightens concentration and alertness, rejuvenates and
> revitalizes unhealthy cells, slows down the aging process,
> and helps depression.
>
> —SHARI ROSE SHEPHERD

Wear a pedometer, a little digital device that records the number of steps you take during your waking hours. It takes about
10,000 steps a day for a person to maintain fitness. That can be
divided into 10 minutes of exercise three times a day, or any other

combination, and include gardening, running after your kids, or climbing stairs with a load of laundry. I've found wearing a pedometer helps me be aware how active or sedentary I am on a particular day and encourages me to get out and move my body if I've been at the computer or in the car too much.

Find out what works for you. I admit it, I'm passionate about exercise because I've seen it make a world of difference in my own life and the lives of countless people I've gotten to know while walking at the mall or in 9-degree weather when we lived in Maine or in the various other neighborhoods we've lived in during the last 25 years.

But if you find walking boring, you could do an exercise video while your kids nap, ride a stationary bike or treadmill at home (you can find them at garage sales for $50 and up), take bike rides as a family, or attend step aerobics at the YMCA. I've found that if you make exercise fun you're more apt to do it. Different seasons of life can produce different needs. I have played tennis with a weekly group, gone swimming with my kids in the summer, and ridden a bike in the basement when freezing rain kept me inside.

What matters is get moving and keep it up for a lifetime! You, your children, and your husband will be so glad you did.

QUESTION FOR REFLECTION
What is your favorite form of exercise? Are you a social exerciser and, thus, need a partner? Or do you like to exercise by yourself?

24

Lord, Change Me

When Chris was 10 years old, we seemed to clash at every turn. I found myself becoming critical of his attitudes and messy room. He was angry that we hadn't gotten him the latest fashion, a pair of black parachute pants we thought he didn't need. He scowled at me at the breakfast table and shut the door to his bedroom. He was irritated with my reminders to clean up his room and stop bugging his sister. I wished he would talk to me, and he clammed up. Most of all, I wanted him to know how much I loved him, and yet irritations pushed us further apart.

So I began to pray. (That's one of the wonderful things about parenting—it draws us to God time and again.) And the more I prayed for our son, the more I heard God say, You're *the one who needs to change. You need to accept Chris just as he is. Don't merely tolerate him, but enjoy and appreciate him, 10-year-old quirks and all! There's a time for correction, but this is a time for acceptance.*

Over the next few weeks, I prayed, *Lord, change me! Forgive me for being irritable, and help me to be the loving, accepting, and understanding mom my son needs. And help me to see him through Your eyes.*

As God gradually answered that prayer, He worked in both of

us. I saw anew some of Chris's wonderful character qualities—his steady study habits and responsibility about school, the attitude of sportsmanship that made him such a great team player in sports. And even a smile or two passed my way. God's Spirit brought a repentance in me concerning my critical attitude and lack of acceptance for people, and He did some refining in my character.

Chris and I played some rounds of Ping-Pong and threw the Frisbee at the park. Even though I had a hard time keeping up with him, my 10-year-old began to share a few of his thoughts with me. I began to understand the things that were bothering him and saw better how to pray for him.

When you understand third-grade math, you don't belong in third-grade math classes. If we understood what parenthood has to teach us, we wouldn't belong in parenthood. If we understood how to be perfect spouses, we probably wouldn't belong in marriage... If we understood our oneness with God we probably wouldn't need churches. Jeremiah envisioned such a day, "When no one shall teach his neighbor saying, 'know ye the Lord,' for they shall know me, from the least of them to the greatest." Meanwhile, thank goodness for the learning.

—POLLY BERRIEN BERENDS

While we were together one day, I remembered the saying "Kids need love the most when they are the most unlovable." I thought how that's just the way God treats us. Long before we loved Him, He loved us and gave His life for us. And He wants to mold us and shape us to become more and more like Jesus. And while the Lord uses us as parents to shape and mold our kids' character, He also uses our children to shape and refine us.

QUESTION FOR REFLECTION

What is God teaching you at this stage of marriage and motherhood? What areas in your life or character need transforming or refining? Thank Him for the learning process and for His patience as you grow (as most humans do) going three steps forward and two steps back.

If we don't change, we don't grow. If we don't grow, we are not really living.

—GAIL SHEEHY

25

Jump In!

It's easy to sit on the sidelines as an observer-parent, but distant from the action. Often we moms find ourselves waiting in the car for the piano or karate lesson to be over or consumed with preparing dinner while our children are tugging at us to go outside. I remember days sitting by the local pool, worn out from the morning's work, watching my children happily frolic in the water while I mulled over the laundry awaiting me at home or worked on bill-paying or some other task I'd brought along.

> The cheerful heart has a continual feast.
>
> —PROVERBS 15:15

One summer when we were living in Maine, I'd driven to the beach where I was glad to be able to stretch out in my striped beach chair and read while our kids played and swam. It takes a conscious effort to dive into those cold, 50-degree Maine ocean waves, just as it takes a conscious effort to get involved with your kids in their everyday playtime activities.

That day, I realized it was a golden opportunity to join my kids in something they truly enjoyed. That in all the hours of going our separate ways in work, school, scouts, or sports, this might be the only chance I'd have today for close, personal involvement in my kids' lives.

Seize it! my heart said.

It's too cold! my body answered.

But by taking the plunge (after getting used to the freezing water), I made great memories with my kids—memories of jumping the waves, of the sandy peanut-butter-and-jelly sandwiches, of laughing at the sea gulls that dive-bombed our food, of the sea shells we collected and brought home in a coffee can.

> Let the children laugh and be glad. O my dear, they haven't long before the world assaults them. Allow them a genuine laughter now. Laugh with them, till tears run down your faces—till a memory of pure delight and precious relationship is established within them, indestructible, personal, and forever.
>
> —WALTER WANGERIN

It is in such moments of shared activity that a strong, loving parent-child relationship is built. Along with all the meals, tasks, and happenings of everyday family life, together times form and cement a solid foundation for learning and life. Times of "being there," in play or activity, not preoccupied with adult worries and concerns but really observing, listening, and being involved, tell a child with your actions, "I love you. You're important enough to warrant my presence and my full attention."

Nowadays, "jumping in" for me means playing the part of Captain Hook while our granddaughter Caitlin is Peter Pan, or acting as the troll while she plays the parts of the Three Billy Goats Gruff stomping across the bridge. She has a great imagination, and mine's getting a little better from her influence. It's throwing a Nerf ball with little Noah or Caleb or running through leaves with them.

It is a happy talent to know how to play.

—RALPH W. EMERSON

Whether it's on Saturday, Sunday afternoon, or in the evenings, look for moments you can "jump in" with your child. Seize these times, and enjoy every minute!

QUESTION FOR REFLECTION

Where is a place you can "jump in" with your child this week?

26

Lord, Give Me Patience

Waiting at the Delta gate in the Colorado Springs airport, I saw a petite, blue-eyed baby girl in a pink-and-yellow gingham bubble suit, matching hat with ruffle, and little pink tennis shoes. When she pulled herself up by a nearby chair, her mother took her hands and, with lots of help and a great display of patience, the baby "walked" through the gate area. Grinning from ear to ear, the little one was so proud. Her feet dragged a little, her gait was unsteady—after all, she was a brand-new walker, at the stage of holding on to things and toddling around but not walking independently yet.

By the smile on her face, you could tell the baby thought she was accomplishing this feat on her own, where all along she was guided by her mother. And when she tired, her tiny hands reached up to mom, who scooped her up just as she fell. So patient with her daughter's stumbles, this young mother didn't rush her. She gently encouraged her along on her little trek.

Isn't that just like how God is with us, I thought—very much with us, patient with our stumbles and mistakes. Ready to pick us up when we fall or encourage us when we drag our feet along the journey.

Oh, that we would be as patient with our kids as God is with us! Patient with their childish mistakes and failures, waiting when they aren't eating or doing something as fast as the rest of the family, and encouraging them when they are behind their peers in sports or school. And not expecting them to be perfect.

Raising children takes lots of patience, and sometimes we moms feel fresh out of it. As Marjorie Holmes wrote, "Oh God, give me patience! With this child who's telling his eager, long-winded story…if I cut him off he'll not only be hurt, he may not come to me with something really important next time. Oh God, give me patience! With this baby who's dawdling over his food…as I wait for a friend who is late, or for a line that is busy, or for traffic to clear."[6]

> As a mother, I must faithfully, patiently, lovingly and happily do my part—then quietly wait for God to do His.
>
> —RUTH BELL GRAHAM

Here are some times when your kids especially need your patience:

When they go through transitions. When kids go through changes, they sometimes stumble, struggle, or even regress. The transition from home to school, the change between elementary school and middle school, or a move across town or across the country can all be difficult. You can help your kids through transitions if you are patient and calm, providing support as they learn the new skills required of them, find their footing, and make the adjustments needed to thrive in the new environment. You can be encouraging if the report card at the end of the first grading period isn't what you'd hoped for and avoid demanding that your child do perfectly in everything, understanding that she may do better in some subjects than others.

When they are preschoolers. Sometimes as moms we expect far too much emotional and mental maturity of preschoolers who are larger physically or are verbally precocious. Often we expect younger kids' behavior to match that of their older siblings, and we hurry them to carry more responsibility or produce more achievements than they're able. It takes a lot of patience to see little kids at the age and stage they really are, not "just like big brother" or little adults, and to rejoice in where they are.

Dr. Louise Bates Ames tells us one of the best things we can do for preschoolers: "Respect individuality. Respect immaturity. Respect your child for what he or she is now, as a preschooler. There may never be a happier time." Read up on the stages of child development, but don't expect your child to develop at the same rate as her siblings or your friends' children. Being aware of the stages kids pass through will help you know what is reasonable so "though your hopes and goals will remain infinitely high, you will be able to wait…to restrain that impulse to push, shove, suggest, insist, and even punish for poor performance or lack of performance."[7]

> Love is patient.
>
> —1 Corinthians 13:4a

When they are late bloomers. I love the children's book *Leo the Late Bloomer* by Robert Kraus. Leo, the main character in the story, can't do anything right. He can't read or write, he can't draw like the rest of the forest creatures, and he eats sloppily while all his friends eat neatly.

"What's the matter with Leo?" asks his dad.

"Nothing," says his mom. "Leo's just a late bloomer."

"Better late than never," thinks his father.

So every day and night Leo's father watches him for signs of blooming. He watches and waits, but still Leo doesn't bloom. Discouraged, he asks, "Are you sure Leo's a bloomer?"

"Patience," mom answers. "A watched bloomer doesn't bloom."

The snow comes and then spring, and Leo's dad is no longer watching as Leo is having a wonderful time playing, exploring, and growing.

"Then one day, in his own time," the author tells us, "Leo bloomed!"

Now Leo can read, write, and draw with a flourish. He even eats neatly, and when he speaks, it isn't just a word—it's a whole sentence that says, "I made it!"

The message of this terrific book is for each of us, as moms and dads, to have patience with late bloomers and all our children, to believe in them, and to know that just like Leo, in their own time and God's time, they will bloom.

QUESTION FOR REFLECTION

What is an area in which you need to be more patient with one of your kids?

All kids are gifted. Some just open their packages earlier than others.

—MICHAEL CARR

27

Why, Mommy, Why?

Noah, our 10-month-old grandson, pulled out all the packages of chips from the bottom drawer in the kitchen. Then, he discovered the cleaning bottles under the sink, investigated the toy drawers in the next room (which weren't nearly as interesting as what was off-limits in the kitchen), threw all the toys on the floor, and then proceeded to give a quick pull to our big dog Randy's coat. Noah has an inborn obsession for finding out how things work and why, and he goes about it with lots of enthusiasm.

When your child learns to talk, he begins to ask questions, hundreds of them: Why is the rainbow all different colors? Why do we have tears? Where does the snow come from? Why is it cold?

Like Noah, young children are driven to figure out what everything is and what makes those things tick. This is a challenging time for us as moms having to field endless questions (and put lots of stuff back in drawers and cabinets), but it is an important time for our kids and their developing curiosity.

First of all, let's stop and thank the Lord for our kids' questions. They are a God-given mechanism, hardwired into their smart brains for learning and growing. Children are filled with so much wonder and curiosity about everything from roly-poly bugs on the sidewalk to what happens when you smash a banana or break an egg to why they can't fly since birds and airplanes can. So you hear *why, why, why* all day.

When I was teaching high school, I wished my students would ask "Why?" more, but by junior high or high school age, kids typically don't ask much about anything. A researcher went into high schools to observe students and discovered that they ask only 11 real questions in a day besides "When's lunch?" or "What're you doing tonight?" My students asked a few more than that during a lively discussion, but the fact remains, somehow the wonderful curiosity of childhood gets lost along the way.

> A stranger to our planet, every normal child is born curious.
> —DOROTHY CORKILLE BRIGGS

At the end of the day you may be at the end of your rope, too tired and busy to give full attention to a whole string of questions. But remember, your response to your children's questions will be either a "Stop" sign (don't ask, touch, try out, or learn) or a "Go" sign (let's think and talk about this question) that encourages learning.

Of course, every time your kids ask you a question, you can't just stop what you're doing, pull out an encyclopedia, and share the answer, so here are some other ways to handle your child's questions:

- *Say*, "What a great question!"
- *Jot down* the question on a card if you don't know the answer, and next time you're out doing errands, stop by the library and pick up a book or get the librarian's help to find the answer. It will make an indelible impression on your child to know that you value her questions.

- *Ask your own questions.* If you go to the zoo, query your kids to stir up their thinking, like: Why do you think the elephant has a long trunk? Why is this jaguar's coat spotted? Which one of these monkeys is not like the others?
- *Encourage creative thinking.* Every child is creative in some area—one artistically, another with problem-solving skills, another in music, drama, or electronics. Provide the raw materials of creativity such as an art box or colorful bin with colored paper, markers, cardboard tubes, glitter, pipe cleaners, and so on. Add some dress-up clothes and even garage sale finds to make up a creativity center. Then give space and time for thinking and creating out of the box. You'll be helping your kids become all God meant them to be!

Children are islands of curiosity surrounded by a sea of question marks.

—UNKNOWN

If you remember that there are no stupid questions, only ones that haven't been thought through carefully, if you ask for your children's opinions and celebrate their curiosity, if you don't put them down for off-the-wall answers, you will go a long way toward keeping their wonder alive and helping them be excited about learning—not just for the preschool years but into adulthood.

QUESTION FOR REFLECTION
How can you affirm or encourage your children's curiosity and creativity at the stages they are in now?

28

Worry Is Like a Rocking Chair

Scrambling out of bed one Sunday morning, I ran to the bathroom for our six-year-old son's inhaler. As I headed down the hall to his room and heard him making the familiar wheezing sound, I thought, *Oh no, not another asthma attack. He's supposed to start first grade tomorrow.*

> Prayer opens the door to Him who can and will save you from your worries.
>
> —CORRIE TEN BOOM

Despite our best efforts the rest of that day with medication, calls to the doctor, prayers, and apple juice, we had to rush Justin to the emergency room at 10:00 P.M. I worried all the way to the hospital. I worried when the doctor said he'd have to be admitted instead of going home after an adrenaline shot. I worried most of all when the next day the doctor told us that something inside our son's body had to rally—the hospital staff had done every-thing they could do for him.

I know what it's like to worry about kids, and I'm not alone. Over the years, I've talked and prayed with hundreds of women about their fears and concerns for their children. With God's help, I've learned some ways to let go of your worries and trust God with your kids:

> Children live in the present, and they know when we are with them physically but not mentally. By worrying about the past and future, we lose the present and our children don't have us, even when we're around.
>
> —DAVID ELKIND

Hope in God and put your child's hand in His hand. After hear-ing the doctor say his hands were tied and he could do nothing more to help our son that September day, I turned to God. In a chapel a few floors below the pediatric ward, I cried out to the Lord, realizing that although I had dedicated baby Justin to God years ago in a church service, I had clung to him through the years and thought if I tried hard enough, I could keep him safe. God called me to entrust Justin totally to His care. As I bowed my head and put our son's hand in God's hand, the fear and worry that had gripped my heart began to melt away.

The best news I, as a young mother, ever heard (next to the fact that Jesus loves me) is that God wants me to cast my cares and bur-dens upon Him. As 1 Peter 5:7 says, "Cast all your anxiety on him because he cares for you." It means that He not only wants me to entrust my three children to His care but that He invites me to tell Him what I am most worried and stressed about and let go, trust-ing that He can handle everything. What a friend we have in Jesus!

I found it helpful to write down the problems or people I was worried about and, one by one, give them to Him in prayer. Just like wrapping them in a package, I handed over my biggest concerns at the throne of grace. Sometimes I had to release the problem 10 times a day as those worries crept back into my thoughts. (Our minds are like tape recorders, and anxious thoughts can play over and over.) But when I let go to the point that I was not thinking about the problem, that was often the point when a creative solution occurred to me or the situation was resolved. And best of all, while I waited for God's answer to come, I had renewed energy to be the mom my kids needed and enjoy the day we had together instead of worrying.

"Worry is like a rocking chair," a wise elderly friend once told me. "It gives you something to do, but it won't get you anywhere."

Do not be anxious about anything, but in everything, by prayer and petition, with thanksgiving, present your requests to God. And the peace of God, which transcends all understanding, will guard your hearts and your minds in Christ Jesus.

—Philippians 4:6-7

Worry is a joy-stealer and energy-robber that causes us to overprotect or control our children and not be emotionally available to them. It also uses up the strength we need for today. "Worrying is carrying tomorrow's burden with today's strength. It's carrying two days at once. It's prematurely thinking of tomorrow," said Corrie ten Boom. I don't know about you, but I need all the strength I can muster just for the next 24 hours.

As moms, we have a desire to protect and care for our children that comes with the job description. But sometimes, that caring can turn to clinging and worry. Here are some things you can do to banish worry:

Call a friend to pray with you. Friendship divides burdens and multiplies hope.

Set your mind on God's promises (such as Isaiah 41:10, 2 Timothy 1:7, Jeremiah 31:3, or Isaiah 40:29) instead of "what ifs?" Absorb the promises, pray them, and believe them.

> Happy is the mother who is too busy to worry in the daytime and too sleepy to worry at night.
>
> —ANONYMOUS

Review how faithful God has been in your life in the past—answered prayers, blessings that have come out of difficult times, ways the Lord has intervened or provided. It will start a chain reaction of gratefulness that helps you put your worries in perspective.

QUESTION FOR REFLECTION

What are you most worried about? Let the Lord know your concerns by praying about them.

29

Power Struggle

"Mom, you're just not fair. It's my hair, and I should be able to do whatever I want with it," my teenage daughter Alison said.

"Ali, when you start paying for your own haircuts, then you can choose the color and style," I replied, driving toward the local beauty shop.

It's amazing how a little thing can cause big conflict. A little thing such as my teenage daughter's hair! It had become a power struggle with us. She wanted to be creative—to cut off her long, naturally blonde hair and dye it burgundy. I envisioned a horrid red shade that wouldn't wash out, and since I was the mom, I thought I ought to have a little input.

My daughter disagreed.

I tried to win her over with compliments on the way home about how great her hair looked after it was trimmed and blown dry. She continued to think I was old-fashioned. Tension grew between us over the hair issue.

Strangely, tension also grew between the Lord and me. Frustrated, I asked for some help: *Lord, what do You want me to do? You know what she'll look like with hair that color!*

One morning, soon after my prayer, God seemed to give me

some direction. But it wasn't what I wanted to hear: *Release her hair.*

You mean let her do whatever she wants with her hair? She'll ruin it! I responded. Now the struggle was between God and me, and only His grace could help me to obey His direction.

Finally, one afternoon about a week later when Alison was in the kitchen, I turned to her and said, "Alison, I've decided your hair is yours to do with whatever you want. Your room is, too—we'd prefer you keep it clean, but no more nagging or going in and picking up after you."

With a smile of glee, Ali agreed. While I wasn't thrilled with her messy room or the creative short hairdos she paraded to the breakfast table, my turning responsibility in this area over to her provided one less opportunity for conflict. I did get in trouble with a few of her friends' moms, whose daughters heard about Alison's new-found hair freedom and thought they ought to have the same.

> As a parent you try to maintain a certain amount of control and so you have this tug-of-war…you have to learn when to let go, and that's not easy.
>
> —ARETHA FRANKLIN

I was encouraged one day soon thereafter when I heard Dr. James Dobson say, "I'm convinced the pulling away of adolescents from their parents is divinely inspired." With relief, I realized Alison's attempts to be more independent were entirely normal. It meant I needed to let go a little more—and entrust her to her heavenly Father.

When the power struggle abated on the hair issue, she began experimenting a bit. She did dye it a dark brown and a reddish hue but that only lasted a few days. She didn't like it and changed it back to her natural color. She even cut the hair of a few of her braver friends. Right away, she showed talent, and later, she attended hair design school between her freshman and sophomore years of college. Now she's cutting my hair, her dad's hair, her brother's and sister-in-law's hair, and the hair of many other people. And she's doing a beautiful job.

When conflicts seem to be mounting at your house, consider these things:

Let the line out a little at a time. Think of giving your child independence as similar to fishing with a rod and reel. You let out just a little line at a time. The struggle isn't as fierce, so the line isn't as likely to break. And your child has an opportunity to grow more capable and responsible along the way. Think of how you can "let the line out" for each of your children. List responsibilities you could delegate and a corresponding privilege you could give each of them.

Fathers [mothers], do not exasperate your children; instead, bring them up in the training and instruction of the Lord.
—EPHESIANS 6:4

Focus on the "majors" instead of the "minors" and you'll temper some of the power struggles. Another way of saying this is: Pick your battles wisely! Instead of nagging and trying to control your child concerning every minor issue, save your steam for the really important things. Sometimes as moms we try to press our own desires into the minor areas, such as how our kids look or the appearance of their bedrooms. We end up wearing ourselves out and causing our kids to tune us out in the process.

For each of us, the majors and minors may be different and

will change with the seasons. For example, you might let a younger child choose her own daily school wardrobe, yet hold to the standard of answering adults respectfully. For a teenager, this might mean giving him some leeway in keeping his possessions and room straight, but sticking to the necessity of his being in by curfew as a "major." Think about what areas you can relinquish decision-making to your children and what areas or standards are non-negotiables, then let your kids know these clearly.

QUESTION FOR REFLECTION

In what areas are you experiencing a conflict or power struggle with your child? What may God be wanting to show you or change in you? Ask for His wisdom in knowing how to respond and handle this issue.

I have held many things in my hands and I have lost them all; but whatever I placed in God's hands, that I still possess.

—Unknown

30

Focus on the Donut

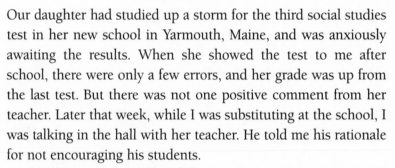

Our daughter had studied up a storm for the third social studies test in her new school in Yarmouth, Maine, and was anxiously awaiting the results. When she showed the test to me after school, there were only a few errors, and her grade was up from the last test. But there was not one positive comment from her teacher. Later that week, while I was substituting at the school, I was talking in the hall with her teacher. He told me his rationale for not encouraging his students.

"I never write 'Good work!' on a test or paper or give an 'A' unless it's a perfect 100—students have to get it all correct to get praise from me," he said with assurance that this must be the right course of action.

Your kids are going to encounter people like this who throw cold water on their enthusiasm or don't affirm them for their efforts. But God has given you, as their mom, the ability to refuel them with doses of encouragement.

One thing I've observed over years of working with children and teens in school and church settings is that a child who lives in an atmosphere of encouragement has a greater chance of succeeding at whatever challenges or tasks he faces. In contrast, those kids who are unmotivated usually had moms and dads who used negative techniques to try to spur a good performance—like withholding praise until the child made an "A" or won the soccer game, overreacting to mistakes, or criticizing. When we do this, we are inadvertently focusing on the hole (what our children are not doing well, what they're lacking) instead of focusing on the donut (what they have accomplished and are doing well). Although these negative responses don't work, parents tend to resort to them when frustrated or disappointed with their kids' performance.

What works a lot better is to focus on the donut: how much your son tried rather than the score, how hard he played rather than whether his team won or lost. Highlighting progress ("Hey, you got 78 on your math test this week. That's five points higher than last week's exam!") is encouraging. Saying, "How could you miss those points again? You knew that material!" is not.

> Anxiety in a man's heart weighs him down, but a good word makes him glad.
>
> —Proverbs 12:25, ESV

If you overlook rather than concentrate on your children's faults and look for something to commend in their character, academic work, music lessons, or other challenges (even cleaning up their rooms or remembering to take out the trash), you'll find that their attitude and effort will improve. You can also encourage by:

Smiles. This sounds so simple, but smiles mean a lot to kids. A smile is an important sign of approval and caring. Children see themselves in the mirrors of our faces, and what they see reflected there can encourage or discourage.

Hugs. Physical affection fills kids' emotional tanks, so hug 'em while you have 'em at home. Countless studies have shown the critical need for babies to be cuddled and held, but the need for physical touch doesn't go away as kids grow. Hugs are needed every day but are especially good for treating problems like bad dreams and disappointments.

> Mothering is the art of bringing kids up without putting them down.
>
> —UNKNOWN

Snapshots. If you give your child little "snapshots" of what he's becoming and the progress he's making, he'll get some vision about how far he can go. "You figured out my computer glitch and fixed it in record time. That's a valuable talent that every company needs" or "You said you'd feed the dog every day this week and you did—that's what I call responsibility!"

During the course of one day, keep track of how many loving, positive words you speak to your child, like "Terrific job," "You're a joy," or "I knew you could do it," and then increase the number tomorrow.

Don't withhold your encouragement until your kids are older, more accomplished, smarter, less messy, or make all "A"s! This is a simple principle, but it will plant seeds of self-confidence and self-worth in your children's life. Focus on the donut—appreciate and encourage them right where they are!

QUESTION FOR REFLECTION

What is the "donut" you could focus on with each person in your family? Consider the efforts they are making to learn something or improve, their creativity, character qualities, skills or talents, spiritual gifts, etc.

31

Tell Me a Story

"Nandy, tell me a story about Mr. Squeeks," said Caitlin, my granddaughter, as we lay on the bed in our guest room. I'd already gotten her a drink of water (twice), she'd gone to the bathroom (again) and wiggled and giggled, and now it was way past 9:00 P.M., when her parents said she had to be asleep.

> Storytelling is an act of devotion…that sends children a clear message: I care so much for you that I want to give you the most precious gift I have—my time. During those moments together, nothing but the story matters.
>
> —CHARLES SMITH

So with the lights dim, I began to spin a story about her imaginary mouse friend, Mr. Squeeks, going to church with Caitlin and the whole family and then to the park for a picnic. I am not as skilled a storyteller as Aesop, but Caitlin, just like most kids, is forgiving about my lapses in plot, helps me along when I forget a detail, and never tires of hearing a story. Within a few minutes, my energetic preschooler began to relax. And when I looked over as I finished the story, Caitlin was fast asleep.

My friend Kay operated a weekly carpool of first through fourth graders, whose antics almost drove her crazy. One October afternoon, in self-defense and to preserve her sanity, she began telling her riders a made-up story called "The Mysterious Bear."

From then on, every Wednesday, her carpool day, the children would ask if she'd tell them the rest of the bear story. They got very quiet (a miracle in itself) and were all ears as she continued the tale of the strange bear. Her son Nick loved the tales so much he asked her to write them down for him, and she did with the agreement that he would write his own original episode.

> I will open my mouth in parables, I will utter hidden things, things from of old—what we have heard and known, what our fathers have told us. We will not hide them from their children; we will tell the next generation the praiseworthy deeds of the LORD, his power, and the wonders he has done.
>
> —PSALM 78:2-4

Storytelling does a lot of great things for almost no cost. It's a way to reestablish communication and a closer bond between kids and parents, as well as relieve stress at the end of the day. You can tell stories in the car on trips or errands, around a campfire, or at family reunions and gatherings. Wherever stories are told, they build a sense of belonging and continuity, especially when you tell family tales about grandma, grandpa, and other relatives. Storytelling ignites kids' imaginations, boosts language skills, and most important, offers the sheer fun and delight of a well-told story.

But I'm not a natural storyteller, you may be thinking. Neither was I.

Here are some suggestions to get started:

Tell personal anecdotes. Your kids will love hearing about when you or dad were little—what your most memorable Christmas was, what trouble you got into, what and whom you played with, your first black eye or stitches, first date, and how you met each other.

Get family members to share a story at holidays when you gather. Looking through old photo albums and asking questions—What was going on in the world when you were a kid? What was life like for you? What songs or movies were popular? Who were your best friends?—will prime the pump of storytelling.

Put your child into the story. For example, my brother George always told his boys "Cowboy Bob" stories, and he'd say, "Cowboy Bob was riding by the ranch and saw Jonathan and Zack. He asked them to go fishing with him and they caught the world's biggest fish!" Kids love being included as one of the characters of the story.

> Sometimes it is the smallest events, the simplest retellings, that touch and change lives. A story that may seem as common as the kitchen sink to me may be the very one that someone else never forgets.
>
> —DEENA LEE WILSON

Tell a round-robin story when you travel together. One person begins the tale, the next person adds more action and maybe a new character, and then the story line passes to the next child or parent.

If you give the gift of storytelling to your children, you may find they become storytellers themselves, passing on the legacy of family history to the next generation.

QUESTION FOR REFLECTION

What's your favorite childhood story—"Cinderella," "The Three Bears," "Thumbelina," or a Bible story like "David and Goliath" or "Daniel in the lions' den"? Practice the story aloud, then surprise your child by telling it some night when the lights are out.

32

Around the Table

"Mom, I'll bet I'm the only guy at my high school who still has dinner every night with his parents," Justin complained as we gathered around the table for yet another family meal. "Most of them just pick up fast food after sports and get to go play video games or watch *Friends* on TV, and I have to be here!"

Truly I don't think we were the only parents and kids eating together that night or any other night. But the truth is, because of parents', children's, and teens' hectic schedules, the family that sits down together nightly for dinner and discussion is becoming more and more rare.

When I grew up as the fourth child among six kids, the dinner hour was a gathering place for the whole family and an occasional neighbor, grandparent, or friend. It was a noisy time of lively conversation, clattering dishes, and a frequent glass of spilled milk, usually mine. It wasn't a perfect time. Some nights we kids squabbled or were grumpy. A few nights I managed to hide my portion of squash or boiled okra—which I found extremely yucky—in my shoe so I wouldn't have to eat it. But the dinner table was where I was exposed to what was going on outside my little world of mud pies and paper dolls. There I heard the neighborhood news, a letter from Alaska where our great-uncle was living, what my big sisters had learned in school, and the results of a political election in Dallas, the city where we lived.

A family dinner hour in which a meal and dialogue are shared at the end of the day has the potential of becoming the center-piece for every family member—youngest to oldest. Granted, it's a challenge to feed babies or toddlers in their high chairs and manage to carry on a coherent conversation, but you can start with a shorter amount of time and lengthen it as they get older.

Although there are lots of places and times you can talk with your kids, a family dinner around the table is one of the best. In fact, studies show children who have a regular family dinner time where they talk with their parents keep a closer connection with them, make higher grades, and achieve more than kids who don't. That's because when students talk about what they're learn-ing, they are able to process, understand, and retain more.

The shared meal is really what you might call a family sacrament. If you're going to have this sacrament, it means somebody's got to help mother—kids, husband—some-body has to help cook and clean up, and that should enrich meals as sacraments because everybody, not just one person, contributes.

—Robert Bellah

Here are some tips to make your family's evening meal a time of enjoyment as well as learning:

Aim for a consistent time, but be flexible. It gives kids a sense of security to know, "We'll all get together at 6:30 and eat." Even if the schedule's interrupted because of an event that comes up, you have a goal to shoot for. As our children got older, we had to plan around Justin's tennis practice, Chris's basketball practice, and Alison's piano or cross-country training, but we aimed to get together as many nights as possible for dinner. If, for a season, you miss evening meals together, have a tradition of Saturday morning pancakes or Sunday brunch.

Eliminate distractions. So you can tune in to each other, turn off the TV and computer. And although this may sound radical, unplug the phone or let the answering machine pick up messages so this short amount of time you have together won't be interrupted. We are asked to turn off our cell phones in church and in movies—why not during family dinner time?

Offer hospitality to one another without grumbling.
—1 PETER 4:9

Encourage your kids to get involved in the discussion. Ask for their opinions, and help even the younger ones feel part of the conversation. The question "What did you learn today?" was a springboard for many interesting discussions at our house. Justin would share about an ethics class debate he participated in on capital punishment. Chris informed us which teams were in the NCAA playoffs. Alison read us a poem she'd written. We talked about school stuff, current events, events coming up.

Avoid negative or unpleasant family business like nagging about problems, handing out discipline for prior behavior, or hashing over how many "C"s one of your kids got on their report card. You can deal with all those things later, but if you consistently talk about them at dinnertime, kids are going to dread getting together. Steer in a positive direction by asking, "What was the *best* part of your day?"

Make it special. The meal doesn't have to be a four-course dinner to be special. Ordinary spaghetti can become extraordinary when you pull out a checkered tablecloth and have a themed dinner night—like Italian. Put a candle on the table and play music. On busy days you can simplify by having pizza, salad, and fruit slices or by using the crock pot—one of the greatest inventions for busy moms. The important thing is being together! Inviting a guest transforms an ordinary meal into something special, and making a centerpiece with flowers, a collection of shells, something seasonal like pretty fall leaves, or finds from a nature walk in a basket brings a center for the conversation. Let your kids help you make a centerpiece.

> A warm welcome is easier when food is always on hand.
>
> —Mimi Wilson

As you gather around the table, thank God together by singing a prayer or letting different members of the family lead the blessing. Don't forget to share cleanup duties. At family mealtimes you'll be passing on important values, building a sense of belonging, and enjoying each other's company all at the same time.

QUESTION FOR REFLECTION

What might you need to rearrange in your schedule to have the evening meal together?

33

Building Your Child's Faith

When Corrie ten Boom was five years old, she learned to read. She loved stories, but especially the ones her mother read to her about Jesus. He was a member of their family, and it was just as easy for her to talk to Him as it was to talk to her mother, father, aunts, or siblings. She always knew Jesus was there.

Every room in the Dutch house of the ten Booms heard prayers, but especially the dining room. Corrie's father sat each day at the oval dining table with his Bible open and had a very natural conversation with the Lord. "Praying was never an embarrassment for us, whether it was with the family together or when a stranger came in. Father prayed because he had a good Friend to talk over the problems of the day; he prayed because he had a direct connection with his Maker when he had a concern; he prayed because there was so much for which he wanted to thank God."[8]

Corrie attended church every Sunday with her family, but it was her home life that had the most impact upon her spiritual foundations, the place where she met Christ and committed her life to Him. It was in a moment of playtime, when five-year-old Corrie was pretending to call on a neighbor. She knocked on a make-believe door, but no one answered.

"Corrie, I know Someone who is standing at your door and knocking right now," said her mother who was nearby watching her. She explained that Jesus said He is standing at the door of her heart, and if she invited Him, He would come into her heart.

At her mother's invitation, Corrie put her little hand in hers and prayed to receive Christ. Soon after, she began having a deep concern for people who were in darkness and, with her mother's encouragement, prayed for them.

> God asks us to do our part in loving our children unconditionally, teaching them the Word of God, and taking them to church. As a mom, I've had to learn to leave the impossible parts to God—I can't change their hearts or give them right thinking or make them love Jesus. That's the Holy Spirit's part.
> —FERN NICHOLS

Children, even at early ages, have very open hearts to God and can, just as Corrie did, experience God's presence in ways that leave an indelible and lifelong impression. Many years later, she survived the horrors of a Nazi prison camp where all of her family members were killed. After that, she traveled around the world until her death, sharing the forgiveness and love of Jesus, impacting millions with the gospel.

Sunday school and church are wonderful and needed in our families' lives, but it is we, as moms and dads, who have the primary responsibility to build the foundations of faith in the lives of our kids so they can learn to know, hear, and listen to God. Here are some ways to do that:

Follow Deuteronomy 6. This key passage for parents tells us to talk about God and His truth "when you sit at home and when you walk along the road, when you lie down and when you get up." It means making God the center and heart of your life and teaching your kids in the everyday circumstances of eating together, putting them to bed, driving in the minivan, dealing with quarrels and school problems, and everything else that happens in a family.

> Jesus said, "Let the little children come to me, and do not hinder them, for the kingdom of heaven belongs to such as these."
>
> —MATTHEW 19:14

Make a Mobile Quiet Time Unit. When you're a mother of small children, you tend to worship God when your kids are asleep, so they never get to see you having special time with God. Then there are those mornings that start with a bang and the children are awake before you, so there's no quiet time with the Lord at all. Connie, a mom I know, made her own "Mobile Quiet Time Unit" by assembling on a tray or basket her Bible and study book, a calendar to jot down things to do that jumped into her mind and distracted her, a prayer journal, and stationery. Then in the morning, while her baby and preschoolers sat on the floor and played, she'd have a few moments to read her Bible and pray. Eventually, the children started getting their own Bibles and joining her.

Lead your children from wonder to worship. Talk about God when you walk through puddles with your kids after a rain. Point out His goodness in the wonder of a sunset. When you kneel by your children's bed to thank God for food, for Jesus, and for all your blessings, you are leading them to worship. They've got the "wonder" part. Young children are filled with a lot of awe and fascination about things like gerbils, snowflakes, Christmas, and lightning bugs. So we can point them very naturally to the God who made all of this for them to enjoy.

> The walks and talks we have with our two-year-olds in red boots have a great deal to do with the values they will cherish as adults.
>
> —EDITH HUNTER

Be intentional about sharing God's Word with them. Doing bite-sized teaching, like taking a verse a week to memorize as a family or reading a psalm or a proverb a day at the breakfast table, are ways to hide God's Word in your kids' hearts. Sing scripture choruses together. And sometime, just for fun, make tunics out of sheets and act out a Bible passage with your kids to help them get the message. You can even have high-chair devotions with your toddlers as you read to them a verse from a beginners' Bible at lunchtime. God's Word never returns void, and He promises it will accomplish the purpose for which He sent it as we teach it to our children. Then pray like crazy for His Spirit to work in your children's hearts and draw them to know and love Him. Through prayer, you can have the greatest influence of all in your children's lives.

QUESTION FOR REFLECTION

What is one thing you can do so that God will be more the center and heart of your family life?

34

Where's God Calling You?

Recently, I heard from my friend Cyndi who for months had been praying about and researching the best high school options in her community for her two daughters. After lots of prayerful consideration, she, her husband, and both daughters clearly sensed that God's leading for the year ahead was the public high school near their home.

Another of my friends decided to home school her daughter again this year for ninth grade, but she's also quite involved in the local public high school, where her son will attend his junior year. Her husband is a school board member for their district.

Yet another mom I know educates all six of their kids at home. Another close friend has her children in a Christian school. She substitute teaches there occasionally to keep in touch with what's going on, sensing that this is God's leading for their family.

As I speak to women around the country, one of the most frequent questions I hear is "Where should I send my kids to school: Christian, public, home school? Should we do preschool or wait? How can I know what is God's best?" This is a big issue for moms today.

Although I wouldn't try to convince you to put your children in a certain kind of school, I can offer some suggestions for making your own decision:

Seek God. Over and over I've seen that where God guides, He provides. At the school He calls you to, whether it's in a building or in your kitchen, He will provide grace right there. We all want our kids to be safe and happy, to learn and become what the Lord intends them to be. But the best place is the place where God directs you and desires you to be for His purposes and your good. I can't tell you where that is, and neither can anyone else, but I can assure you that if you seek God, if you pray as a family and as parents about the issue, He will show you and light your path. It's a promise.

> Call to me and I will answer you and show you great and unsearchable things you do not know.
>
> —JEREMIAH 33:3

Remember, there's no perfect school. Oh, how we wish there were a perfect school where our children would be happy every day and make good grades and love every teacher and have friends that are good influences. But on this side of heaven, I've found, there are no perfect schools. I've looked! Schools are run by imperfect people with usually good intentions, attended by imperfect children with imperfect parents. And each schooling option is going to have its challenges and problems—plus its benefits and blessings.

Granted, public schools have some even larger issues for Christian families: such as mandatory Islam instruction and teaching on homosexuality in California schools, violence, or liberal sex education. I don't minimize these, because they are huge issues.

But we can't generalize that "every public school is this or that" because every school is different (so are Christian schools and home schools). You have to look at each individual school and the character and beliefs of the faculty, administrators, and parents. Don't just look at a brochure or video about the school. Interview the principal. Talk to teachers and other parents. Sit in on classes as an observer (make an appointment first), and ponder as you watch what's going on: Could my child thrive and learn in this environment? Is this where God wants my child? If He says, *This is the right public school or Christian school*, know that you aren't just putting your children there. It's a mission for the whole family. If it's home schooling you are led to, God will give you grace and help you find the great support groups and resources that are available.

> Neither public, Christian, nor home schooling is any more or less "spiritual." God calls us to different areas and challenges. And in any situation, He will use problems to conform us to the image of Christ.
>
> —DOROTHY BURSHEK

Be involved. Wherever God calls you to put your kids for each year of school, remember you are delegating only part of your children's education. You are still the director of their schooling, an integral part of the process, and you need to be involved.

How? Pray for the teachers, classmates, principals, and your child. (Visit momsintouch.org to connect with a prayer group for your child's school.) Build a relationship with the teachers, go to open houses and conferences, and head off problems by being proactive—know what your kids are being taught. Find something you can do to contribute to the overall quality of the school. No matter where your children attend school, as they grow, you won't believe how important and time-consuming the whole education issue becomes. Sometimes you will even feel that *you've* gone back to school!

> The safest place is the center of God's will.
> —BETSIE TEN BOOM

Support, don't judge. If someone in your church or neighborhood has chosen a different schooling option for their children, let me encourage you to respect their different callings and the unique path God has directed them. Don't judge or condemn the fact that they are in a different place than you are. Support your brothers and sisters in other schools with love, encouragement, and prayers. And please pray for the more than 650,000 Christian teachers who are serving in the public schools every year, in the mission field God has called them, some in your own community.

When you drive through a school zone, think of it as a "prayer zone," regardless of whether you have children attending there. Pray that every person will know Jesus, that He will bring them from darkness into His marvelous light, that the students and teachers will be safe and protected, and that God will accomplish His purposes as He strengthens the Christians who are serving there.

QUESTION FOR REFLECTION

Have you sensed God's guidance concerning your children's schooling? Are there others you could support or pray for who have chosen a different option for their kids' education?

35

I Had a Mommy Who Read to Me

As my husband and I drove along Highway 281 through Texas recently, I read a few of the more interesting signs aloud: Houses of Distinction (on top of a Porta Potti), Texas Ranger Museum and Brazos Bell Bluebonnet Festival (both sounded fun but we didn't have time to stop). But these signs didn't compare to one we saw in Bangkok, Thailand: SOFT-DRINKS-INSIDE-TOILET.

Highway signs take me back to some of my earliest memories of childhood. Many Sundays, after my father picked us up from church, he'd drive all six of us kids and Mama from Dallas to Aunt Bess's house in Arlington. Sitting in the backseat with my four sisters, packed like sardines, I gazed out the window as mile after mile went by and I tried to decipher the signs along the road. Only five years old, I hadn't been to school yet. My knowledge of the English language was rudimentary, and what I knew of the "ABC"s came from my big sisters playing school with us "three babies," as we were called. So the signs seemed a great mystery that the "big girls" had already figured out.

All of a sudden, as we passed a small strip shopping center

(big malls didn't exist then), I saw a sign and said, "Saloon! That's *saloon!*" I was very proud of myself. But instead of celebrating my verbal breakthrough, my sisters exploded in laughter.

"No, silly, it's *salon*," they corrected in their big sister way. Even that splash of cold water didn't dampen my thrill over this phonetic awakening.

A burst of joy filled my heart—like fireworks going off. "Salon! Salon!" I read it for myself now and it clicked. Then I read another sign and another. Mom had read me the Bible and little books lots of times. But now the world of words began to open before me and I moved on to Mother Goose stories, Golden Books, and Nancy Drew mysteries before long. Yet highway and street signs still remained fun reading when I had to be in the car.

> You may have tangible wealth untold
> Caskets of jewels and coffers of gold.
> Richer than I you can never be—
> I had a mother who read to me.
>
> —STRICKLAND GILLILAN

All of us take numerous short jaunts in the car for errands and longer ones for vacations or to go see grandma. You can take advantage of those times to play games with highway signs. (Find an *A* in a sign, then a *B, C,* and move on through the alphabet.) Keep track of how many different state license tags you can find on cars. And read some signs out loud as you drive to stir up your little pre-reader's curiosity about the words.

Here are some more ways to encourage your children's reading, even reluctant readers:

Whatever your child is interested in, connect it with reading. Reading is vital to your child's learning—and can be lots of fun if you tap into kids' center of learning excitement, the subject or topic they want to learn about more than anything else. If your child loves sports, get some books on soccer, basketball, or their favorite sport or sports hero. If she is fascinated with whales or clouds and storms, there are great books on those topics. Ballerinas, cowboys, insects—the sky's the limit with the topics available in books.

Take advantage of your local public library. For free you can check out wonderful children's books, educational games, books on tape, and lots more. When summer comes, get your kids signed up right away for the reading contest or program. Most towns and cities have summer programs with prizes and other incentives for reading.

Children are made readers on the laps of their parents.
—EMILIE BUCHWALD

If you go to the library at least every two weeks and get a big stack of books, you can deposit them in baskets in obvious places, such as by the couch or your child's bed. Don't put the books out of sight, or they'll be out of mind. When our three children were growing up, I'd get at least 25 or more books every two weeks. Let your kids pick out their favorites, but also look for colorful books that push their center of learning excitement and help them get hooked on reading.

Play games that include reading, like Boggle, Password, Go to the Head of the Class, Scrabble Junior, and others.

Take your child to a local bookstore to spend her birthday or Christmas money on a book by a favorite author rather than a new electronic toy.

Install a clip light next to your child's bed, or provide a bedside lamp and interesting books. Then give her a little extra time to read in bed each night before lights out.

Cuddle up with your kids and a book. Reading aloud as a family is one of the best ways to encourage your children's reading and produces priceless memories. Chapter books are especially fun, because kids have to wait till the next night for the next episode. Get one of the Chronicles of Narnia series books by C.S. Lewis, an E.B. White book like *Charlotte's Web*, or *Little House on the Prairie* by Laura Ingalls Wilder, and you'll make some wonderful reading memories together.

Every season brings a reason to share reading as a family and boost your child's love of books. Read aloud by the fireplace, while traveling, or while kids recover from the flu. Make library trips at any time of year. Read recipes together while baking Christmas cookies—whatever the time or place, reading is a foundation for life.

QUESTION FOR REFLECTION
What is your child's center of learning excitement? Get books on that topic to spark his reading.

36

Christmas Is Coming

One Christmas we were in Maine, 2,000 miles away from the family and friends we usually celebrated the holidays with. With no prospect of visitors, and knowing few people in the town where we lived, the whole family was a little blue. One day the week before Christmas, I decided to call a local university's international students office to see if there was a foreign student who had no plans for the holidays.

I explained what I was looking for to the receptionist, a girl with a distinctly Chinese accent, and asked, "Would you know of a student who'd like to spend Christmas weekend with an American family?"

"Oh, I do! I will come!" she replied. "I would be in dormitory by myself, for students are going home and my family is 10,000 miles away in Shanghai."

So the Friday before Christmas, we drove into Portland to pick up Zhu Hong. She'd been in America for a semester but hadn't seen the inside of an American home. Having grown up in Communist China, Zhu Hong, excited to celebrate her first Christmas, met us at her dorm with a wide smile.

After ice skating with our kids and helping us make sprinkle cookies, Zhu Hong sat at the table with us for our Christmas Eve meal and then entered right into our family traditions of candle lighting, caroling, opening gifts (including her first Bible), and reading the story of the first Christmas from the book of Luke together.

Rather than being a lonely holiday, it turned out to be one of our happiest. God used that Christmas to cause me to think about what's important. He infused our customs with new meaning as we shared them with a new friend from across the world.

No matter what month of the year you are reading this chapter, as fast as time goes, it is not going to be long until Christmas. Since you aren't yet in the thick of the holiday bustle, it's the ideal time to think about what really matters in the holiday.

> I bring you good news of great joy that will be for all the people. Today in the town of David a Savior has been born to you; he is Christ the Lord.
>
> —LUKE 2:10B-11

"All I want for Christmas is my two front teeth" goes an old familiar Christmas song. An informal survey of moms and dads shows that what grown-ups want is different—it's two more weeks to prepare for Christmas!

For several years, we lived near a big mall, which gave me a new perspective of how crazy the Christmas frenzy is. The mall was decorated to the hilt, and opportunities abounded to spend money (or use the credit card, which financial counselors tell us people usually don't pay off till the next Christmas and beyond).

It's inevitable: Christmas is coming. How are you going to spend it? What really matters? What makes lasting Christmas memories? College students were surveyed about their holiday memories and what they remembered best. Not one mentioned presents. That may be hard to imagine when your kids want a new PlayStation or other toy they saw on TV so desperately they think they can't live without it. But the favorite holiday memories college students rated were: being with grandparents, being with family, decorating the tree, singing carols, eating a special meal.

In another survey, 15,000 kids around the country were asked, "What makes a happy family?" At the top of the list wasn't designer jeans or new video games but doing things together. Doing things together as a family can naturally evolve into traditions and become a way of building continuity and security. Traditions are also part of the glue that holds families together. They create memories that last a lifetime.

> The spirit of Christmas brings memories drifting down like snowflakes.
>
> —DOROTHY COLGAN

Here are a few favorite Christmas traditions which are low-stress and inexpensive but yield a high return on warm memories:

Share a Christmas classic. One of the loveliest and easiest traditions is to put your favorite holiday books in a big basket with a festive bow and set it by the Christmas tree or fireplace to be enjoyed by all. Having the basket of Christmas classics close by, you'll be encouraged to sit down and read a story to your children. Our basket started with an old copy of *The Littlest Angel* from my childhood, and each year I added a new Christmas book: *A Cup of Christmas Tea* by Tom Hegg, *Polar Express* by Chris Allsburg, *The Best Christmas Pageant Ever* by Barbara Robinson, and others. Our kids are grown, but now I'm reading

the Christmas books to our grandchildren, and I still add a new
one to the collection each year.

Make a Christmas photo album. Our kids always headed for
this album when they came home from college. They enjoyed
looking through it and remembering Christmases past. The
album is a special place to keep all of your Christmas keepsake
photographs—we started ours with a few old pictures of my husband and me under our own childhood trees, our first Christmas
as newlyweds, the children's first Christmases, school and church
plays, friends and family who joined us for holiday gatherings,
our tree-trimming nights, etc.

> The best Christmas gift of all is the presence of a happy
> family all wrapped up with one another…in love.
>
> —UNKNOWN

No matter how busy we are or how grown up our kids
become, we all spend some time perusing the Christmas album
each holiday season. Take a standard or large photo album, and
cover it with a bright holiday fabric. Embroider the word *Christmas* diagonally across the front if you're good with a needle (or
sewing machine), fill with photos, and enjoy year after year!

Keep Christ in Christmas. Look up a few verses on each of the
names of Jesus, such as the Light of the World, the Door, the
Bread of Life, the Living Water, Savior, Lord, Emmanuel, and read
the verses as a family around the dinner table each evening.

Write Santa letters. Write special letters of appreciation and
love for your children. Place the letters in their stockings. Include
little reminders of the past year, like how proud you are of the
progress your child has made or a character quality you've seen
developing. Write the letters on decorative paper with a border

(available at copy shops or office supply stores), and enclose in envelopes. These special letters will become one of the favorite stocking stuffers at your house.

Give intangible gifts, like the gift of an open door, of encouragement, or of prayer. Look around for new folks on the block or in your neighborhood, or find an international student at a local university. Invite them for hot cocoa and cookies or to accompany you to a Christmas play or event at church. Give the gift of encouragement by finding someone to compliment or affirm, such as a waiter in a restaurant or a friend who was thoughtful. Finally, take a pocketful of time to offer special Christmas prayers for your children, neighbors, friends, and those you care about. Your prayers will make an eternal difference and be a gift that will last far beyond the holiday season.

If you find yourself in a whirlwind, getting stressed or exhausted, take 15 minutes to take some deep breaths or sip a cup of tea. Reread the Christmas story from Luke 2, and think on the One whose birthday you're about to celebrate. As you do, you'll find yourself refreshed and ready to enjoy the rest of the season.

QUESTION FOR REFLECTION

What are your favorite Christmas memories from childhood or your current family's holidays? What traditions do you want to keep, and which ones should you let go of because they are too stressful?

37

Mentors for Moms

Flo sat at my kitchen table as I served her raspberry tea and slices of homemade banana bread. I wasn't great at baking cookies, but I could whip up a yummy fruit bread or pan of blueberry muffins. We talked about her grandchildren and great-grandchildren (30-plus combined), about my children as they circled around us and played, and about the Lord. Whenever I talked to Flo, Jesus always came into the conversation because He was her best friend.

In little windows of time like these, Flo, a widow of 75, and I, 30, began to develop a friendship. I didn't know until a few years later that the Lord had spoken to Flo's heart after we first met at a prayer meeting I had visited. He had said, "Flo, I want you to bring Cheri and her young family into your circle of prayer and intercede for her just like you do your own daughters."

What an incredible gift her prayers and friendship were! She not only prayed for me, my husband, and my children for as long as she was on earth, but she also taught me to go deeper in prayer. Sensing our spiritual hunger, she invited a few of us young mothers to her home to pray with us. Flo had been going into the Lord's presence for over 50 years, so for her, prayer was as natural as breathing. Somehow, she took us on her wings before the throne of grace, and without teaching, in the very act of praying honestly, humbly, and perseveringly, she taught us a great deal.

Flo was also the first person who recognized some potential in a few little poems I'd written and shared with her. "You could be a writer, honey. God could use you to encourage people and give them hope," she said on one of our first afternoons together. She prayed for every book I wrote and every group of people I spoke to, and she was an incredible cheerleader along the way.

And when my teens went through a few rough waters in adolescence, Flo helped me gain perspective, reminding me again and again to roll all my burdens for them over to the Lord. She prayed my daughter Alison and her fiancé right up to the altar then died peacefully in her sleep the night before their wedding. I watched her reach out to neighborhood kids who didn't know Jesus, pray for the many people God had laid on her heart, and give out of a joy that only comes from loving and abiding in Jesus, even when she could no longer drive because of surgery and old age.

> [The older women] can train the younger women to love their husbands and children, to be self-controlled and pure, to be busy at home, to be kind . . .
>
> —Titus 2:4-5

How thankful I am for this precious, godly woman God brought into my life! It was His way of equipping me to be the wife and mother He wanted me to be. As Titus 2:4 explains, older women are to mentor young women, showing them how to love their husbands and kids and care for their homes.

My mother was also a great mentor to me as I watched her

through the years, caring for the six of us, yet reaching out to people in need, exercising her gift of hospitality in our home.

Mama has been gone two decades, but her sayings have mentored me through the years. For example, "Busy hands are happy hands" encouraged me to keep an art box in the kitchen so the kids could draw while I was cooking. "Cleanliness is next to godliness" is not in the Bible, but Mama lived by it. How, with six kids, she kept the house clean and every stitch of clothing and bedding laundered, folded, and put away before bedtime is beyond me. But I suspect her saying "A place for everything and everything in its place" was part of it.

God has also used other women in my life. Some of these older mentor moms were in my life for only a season. Like Ray, a 90-year-old woman in our neighborhood years ago who, though almost totally blind, was interested in other people and kept up with new ideas and current affairs by listening to countless books on tape. Ray was a living demonstration of how to enjoy life and family in the midst of limitations and disappointments. We had wonderful book discussions during the two years I knew her, and she always kept a candy jar out for my children and those neighborhood kids who dropped by.

Mentoring moments may not be prolonged, but when someone whom you respect says just the right words or gives you the attention when you need it the most, that effect can last a lifetime.

—BETTY SOUTHARD

Billie, my college friend Melina's mom, treated my kids as if they were her grandkids (their own grandparents weren't in town). Though an invalid for most of the years we were friends,

Billie offered me a mother's accepting and understanding heart and whispered hope with her gentle words when I most needed it.

Patty remembered my birthday every year, shared her wisdom, took time to have an occasional lunch with me, and prayed for me. When I was feeling a bit over the hill as I approached my 50th, she told me I was about to enter my prime, the best years of a woman's life she called the "Fabulous 50s." And you know what? She was right!

> Many of those who have gone before us—our moms, mothers-in-law, and others—are master teachers. If we are not learning from what they have to offer, we are missing out on one of the greatest resources available to us, especially for those of us who are just embarking upon this journey of motherhood.
>
> —LESLIE PARROTT

How good of God to give me these spiritual moms who mentored me as a mother, wife, and Christian—especially since my own mother died at age 59. He doesn't have spiritual moms in the Body of Christ just for me, but for you as well—mentors who can encourage, nurture, and help you learn and grow on your journey of mothering.

Mentor moms also...

- help us gain a bigger picture of family, children, and life;
- ease our fears and encourage us to trust in the faithfulness and love of God when things look dark; and
- help us appreciate the season we and our children are in.

How can you find these women? Mentoring programs in churches are great and can help you find an older mom to build a relationship with. But in my experience, it can also happen without a structure or program as you trust God to lead you across the path of a potential mentor. Here are some ways to start:

Look around you in your church, neighborhood, and circle of acquaintances. Don't leave out your mother, mother-in-law, or grandma, who may have a wealth of things to impart to you.

Is there an older woman you feel drawn to or would like to get to know? Invite her over for tea or lunch, or ask if you could meet for coffee some day. Let her know you'd like to get to know her, then see what the response is. Most older moms are thrilled when someone initiates spending time together. Whatever age you are, there's an older woman who is five or 10 years or more down the road who can hold out a light—and perhaps would welcome a friendship.

If your mom has died or you live hundreds of miles away from her, ask God to show you the spiritual mothers in the body of Christ He has prepared for you to be a blessing to, and who would be willing to come alongside you.

Be teachable. If they don't think they know it all, younger mothers can greatly benefit from the wisdom of veteran moms. Open your heart and ask older women for advice on a puzzling parenting or relationship issue you're facing, tell them something you admire about them, or ask for them to pray for you.

As you cultivate a relationship with an older woman, you will find that your life—and hers—will be tremendously enriched, and you will gain insights that can help you become the mom you long to be.

QUESTION FOR REFLECTION

Is there a particular issue you have insight into that you could pass along to another mom? Or is there an issue about which you'd love to have the perspective of an older mother? Take the initiative to encourage a mom younger than yourself, and pray for God to bring a wise older woman along your path.

38

No Perfect Parents

A few years ago, when my friend Karen's son Christopher was three years old, she and her husband, Jim, got the chance to fly to Singapore to visit her sister, who was living there at the time. It was a fascinating time to be there, because it was only weeks after the American teenager was arrested and caned by the authorities as punishment for having been caught stealing. The uproar from America over this brutal Asian practice was just settling down when they arrived.

Jim and Karen were more concerned, however, about their trip and their child than they were about this international event. But what an angel Christopher was on the plane ride over—he exceeded all his parents' expectations for good behavior! Since it was a night flight, he slept most of the time, and when he was awake, he played and giggled. As first-time parents, they were so proud of their little boy. They had heard stories of how difficult it is for some small children to travel and were extremely thrilled that their boy was so well behaved. They were even patting themselves on the back for overseeing such a smooth trip.

The two weeks in Singapore, Thailand, and Indonesia were a fantasy. The Covells rode elephants, boats, rickshaws, and bicycles, and Christopher joined in almost everywhere. By the time the three of them got back to the Singapore airport, Karen and Jim were commenting on how easy it was to travel with their wonder boy! It had been an incredible experience for all of them and, in fact, Jim and Karen were feeling pretty good about themselves as mommy and daddy.

All of you, clothe yourselves with humility toward one another, because, "God opposes the proud but gives grace to the humble."

—1 PETER 5:5

After the family arrived at the airport and checked in, they soon joined a large group of American senior citizens who were on the same plane, also returning from an exciting Asian trip. The elder travelers were in great spirits from their trip as well, but seemingly hungry to talk to a young American family. These lovely, older people poured all their attention on Christopher as everyone waited for the plane. He was in an exceptionally good mood and was eating up all the attention. With a warm audience, the three-year-old talked, jumped, made faces, and smiled. The whole group had truly bonded by the time they were told to board the plane. Christopher got hugs, pats on the head, and wonderfully kind words as each member of the group passed him. And Jim and Karen got more compliments than they ever could have imagined about how good, cute, and well behaved their little boy was!

Then reality hit. Jim and Karen were on the plane for only a few minutes when suddenly, their angelic child had had enough. Right after the plane took off and the flight attendants were passing out hot washcloths to prepare the passengers for the long trip,

Christopher had an all-out temper tantrum! He wanted to have a tray table to play with, but his row of seats didn't have them. This became the most important thing in the world for him, and instantly, the dam broke. He screamed and hollered to get his own tray table.

Accept me—for what I am
Not what I could have been
  or even will be.
Accept me—so I need not twist myself
  to fit your pattern…
But resting in acceptance,
  can grow.

—RUTH REARDON

Immediately, people started looking over at the Covells and their "out of control" boy. Some of the elderly people made comments about this loud, badly behaved child. As Karen heard comments like "I hope he doesn't do that the whole way back" and "I wish his parents could control him a little better," she began feeling quite embarrassed and ashamed as the mother of the troublemaker. But the comments continued, and the piercing looks were worth much more than a thousand words.

In a full plane, it was impossible to get Christopher what he wanted, and Karen panicked as she tried to settle down this angel-turned-demon of a little boy. Jim and Karen both tried to distract him, hold him, and finally clamp down on him as he cried and yelled. But they missed one arm. Just then, the stewardess stopped by their seats and handed Jim a wet, hot washcloth. Before Karen could take the washcloth being held out to her, Christopher grabbed it and threw it as hard as he could in front of him. The washcloth soared over three rows of seats and landed on the head of one of the senior citizens from the American tour group!

At that moment, one of the other old men sitting on the aisle two rows up, turned around, amidst the murmuring of unhappy people, and said almost under his breath, "Now I see why they cane people here!"

That did it. The Covells had been betrayed. The world was against them, and all pride as a parent was zapped out of Karen instantly. She was clearly out of control, she was a failure, and her child was hopeless. The three of them were alone, abandoned by all other supposed friends and supporters, and there was an angry man with a wet head three rows up. All Karen could do was to hang on to Christopher and wait for the storm to pass.

It finally did a few minutes—or was it a few hours—later. They pulled themselves together, apologized to the wet-headed gentlemen in front of them, and tried not to make faces at all the old people around who were still glancing menacingly at them.

There are no perfect families.

—KEVIN LEMAN

Later on into the flight, after that horrible incident, Jim and Christopher were both napping. Karen thought about what a great parent she had thought she was a few hours ago. It didn't take long for her to realize that Christopher's fantasy trip wasn't because she was such an incredible mother but because he was having a wonderful time.

Suddenly, Karen understood how easy it was for her to take credit for something that she really had nothing to do with. In fact, she wouldn't know what kind of parent she really was until

Christopher was old enough to make his own decisions and live his own life. Until then, the jury would be out, and she and Jim would have to humbly seek God in everything they did. She saw how little control she has of anything and how much she needed the Lord to keep her on track as she and Jim walked together on the complicated and humbling journey of parenthood. She vowed never again to give herself credit for those glorious moments when their children (now two boys) acted like angels. Karen reflected that while she wanted to stay thankful for the peaceful moments, she also wanted to remember that the little demons sitting on her boys' other shoulder are ready to strike.[9]

Such devastating moments are going to hit most moms at some point in their kids' lives. How can you respond? And how can you avoid the pitfall of perfectionism?

Put away the myth. The perfect parent/perfect child concept is a myth. The only perfect parent was and is God, and look at the trouble He had with His kids, Adam and Eve! If you aim for perfection in your children and your parenting skills, you will be very disappointed when you or they don't meet those expectations. You can depend on God's grace to be the parent your children need, so keep asking Him for His wisdom, and be thankful when your kids' behavior makes you happy!

Avoid the compulsive drive for perfection. When perfectionist parents put pressure on their kids, they tend to become little perfectionists who are excessively driven, become prisoners of their own expectations, and underachieve. Help your child accept that humans make mistakes—lots of them—and let her hear you acknowledge your failures without acting like it's the end of the world. ("Oh, I goofed on that project, but it's okay. I can figure out a different way to make it work" or "I remember one time I made a low grade on a test.")

Cultivate a sense of humor in yourself and your child. As Karen and Jim look back on their humbling airline experience with Christopher, they can chuckle about the whole scene. It's hard to have a sense of humor in a stressful moment! But humor can help overcome the drive for perfection and relieve stress. It allows you to laugh in a friendly way at your own and your kids' mistakes, and it helps you avoid becoming overly serious about everything that happens.

QUESTION FOR REFLECTION

Are you—or your child—consistently worried and anxious about doing things perfectly or afraid of failure? If so, bring this to God and ask Him to give you both a fresh perspective and reassurance to gain a more realistic view of yourself, your child, and others.

39

If I Had My Life to Live Over

I was struck this week by something that Len LeSourd, second husband of beloved author Catherine Marshall, wrote after her death: "I have one major regret about all this. We didn't take enough time to smell the flowers, to learn what it really means to take a vacation. We went from deadline to deadline, from crisis to crisis, dealing with what had to be done, forgetting too often to mark on our calendar those letters F U N. I feel deeply convicted about this, but the truth is that Catherine and I were workaholics."

Ouch. I can definitely identify with the need to take a break and smell the flowers. It's so easy to be preoccupied with tomorrow's project or next week's problem until you feel overwhelmed and all your energy is wasted before you get there! It's easy to put off fun because, like Catherine Marshall, you've become a workaholic.

It reminds me of what Erma Bombeck said when she was battling cancer: "If I had my life to live over, I would have talked less and listened more. I would have invited friends over to dinner even if the carpet was stained and the sofa faded. I would have eaten the popcorn in the 'good' living room and worried much less about the dirt when someone wanted to light a fire in the fireplace…burned the pink candle sculpted like a rose before it melted in storage. I would have sat on the lawn with my children and not worried about grass stains. Instead of wishing away nine months of pregnancy, I'd have cherished every moment and realized that the wonderment growing inside me was the only chance in life to assist God in a miracle. I would seize every minute…look at it and really see it…live it…and never give it back."[10]

If there were one thing I could change about family trips in my childhood, it would be that instead of just driving by a mountain or forest and seeing it through the car window, I would have experienced it with hiking, touching, and exploring.

—KATHY SVEJKOVSKY, 20

"What would I have done differently in my 20s and 30s if I had known then what I know now?" asked a 40-year-old mom. "I would have laughed more, seen more Laurel and Hardy movies… I would have taken more time to note the changing seasons. ('Can you believe it?' an elderly friend asked me one spring day. 'Can you believe that even if I live to be 100, I will see all this only 100 times?') I would have understood sooner how profoundly satisfying the ordinary transitions of daily life can be: the perfect cup of morning coffee, the son shouting down 'Good night!' from his room, the ginger-colored cat caught napping in a triangle of sunlight."

As I was pondering these thoughts, I considered what I'd do differently if I could go back and begin my family again. I think I would start with two words: slow down. Also, I'd give more backrubs to my kids after lights out instead of rushing back to the dishes or papers I had to grade. I'd have dealt with some unresolved grief and loss issues from my past sooner so my heart would be lighter. And I, too, would laugh more.

> Since our time at home is short, let's make the most of the summer. Then armed with positive memories, we can embrace more fully the world beyond our doorstep. We can dance into a winter of rich reward, rather than shuffle into a season of regret.
>
> —BRENDA HUNTER

I don't know what responsibilities you're juggling, what deadlines you're facing, or what you're preoccupied with. I always seem to be facing one deadline or another as a writer. But let me encourage you to take these thoughts to heart and...

Talk with your family about the one thing you don't want to miss doing this summer or spring or fall, and then just do it.

Find a way to show or tell each member of your family how much you love them. Say encouraging words to those you meet.

Invite someone over for dinner even if the carpet has a stain or the décor in your house isn't just the way you want it. Light some candles.

And don't forget, before you tuck your kids into bed, thank God together for the happy moments.

QUESTION FOR REFLECTION

What would you have done differently in your 20s or 30s (or in the last five years) if you knew what you know now? What would you like to do differently *today*?

40

Keeping Our Focus (A Last Word to Moms)

As I finish this book, I am in a rustic cabin a block from the beach on Galveston Island. I had visions of walking along a pristine stretch of sand and watching the ocean on my breaks. However, the first thing I encountered after arriving was the stinkiest pile of seaweed I have ever seen. Not one pile, but miles of it. A storm had brought the seaweed in the weekend before, and here it lay being heated up by the summer sun, making the odor worse.

At first, all I could see or smell was that stinky seaweed. I shortened my walk so I didn't have to endure it, and I was so frustrated that the beach crews hadn't cleaned it up, I didn't even notice the beautiful things about the day. The next morning, I went out and there the seaweed was, still lying on the beach as far as I could see.

But this time I chose to focus on something else: the dazzling blue Texas sky, the little toddler with blonde ringlets who smiled at me and said, "Hi!" as I passed her. A dad and son making the most elaborate sand castle I'd ever seen, surrounded of course with seaweed; it didn't seem to dampen the artists' creativity. Fish jumping in the glittering water. My steps lightened as a cool breeze of thankfulness blew through me. Oh, the seaweed was still there. It just wasn't commanding my full attention because my focus was somewhere else.

Life is not a beach. But there often is a lot of stinky seaweed in our lives as moms—things we didn't plan on happening, sickness, layoffs, difficult days, and conflict to resolve.

But God wants us to look up and keep our focus on the call and the prize. What is it? "I press on to take hold of that for which Christ Jesus took hold of me... But one thing I do: Forgetting what is behind and straining toward what is ahead, I press on toward the goal to win the prize for which God has called me heavenward in Christ Jesus" (Philippians 3:12-14)—and also not miss the beautiful things He puts along the way in each day.

My prayer is that wherever you are on this journey of mothering, you will receive the mercies the Lord has that are new for you each morning and that His unfailing love will surround you and your children. May your heart be filled with hope and your step be lightened because your gaze is fixed on Him. And may you enjoy the ride!

With much love from my heart to yours,

Cheri

A Note about Discussion Groups

At the end of each chapter you'll find a question for reflection. These questions can be used for individual reflection as well as group discussion. If you are participating in a study group or an informal mom's group, you may want to read and discuss three to six chapters a week. The chapters are short, so most moms can manage a chapter a day. Don't feel you have to discuss every question—Some weeks you may get through only one or two. The idea is to relax and talk about the things that matter to the moms in your group. So whether you're reading this book individually, or you're participating in a discussion group, enjoy becoming the mom you're meant to be!

Notes

1 Leslie Parrott and Mary Beth Lagerborg, *If You Ever Needed Friends, It's Now* (Grand Rapids: Zondervan, 2000), p.21.

2 Stella Chess and Alexander Thomas, *Know Your Child* (New York: Jason Aaronson, 1996), p. 63.

3 John M. Drescher, *Seven Things Children Need* (Scottdale, Pa: Herald Press, 1976), p. 59.

4 Brenda Hunter, *Home By Choice* (Sisters, Oreg.: Multnomah Publishers), 2000.

5 Dr. Ross Campbell, *Relational Parenting* (Chicago: Moody Press, 2000), p. 32.

6 Marjorie Holmes in *A Treasury of Prayer for Mothers* by Helen Allingham (Tulsa: Honor Books, 1996), p. 62.

7 Louise Bates Ames, *Don't Push Your Preschooler* (New York: Harper and Row, 1980), p. 203.

8 Corrie ten Boom, *In My Father's House* (Grand Rapids: Revell, 1976), p. 66.

9 Original story told to Cheri Fuller by Karen Covell, author of *The Day I Met God:* Multnomah Publishers.

10 Erma Bombeck, "If I had my life to live over" (www.robinsweb.com/inspiration/erma.html).

About the Author

Cheri Fuller is a wife, mother, inspirational speaker, and an award-winning author of more than 27 books including the best-selling *When Mothers Pray, Opening Your Child's Spiritual Windows, Opening Your Child's Nine Learning Windows, When Children Pray,* and others. Cheri's desire to renew the hearts of moms and build families has inspired her messages, magazine articles, and books which provide hope and encouragement to women throughout the U.S. and other countries.

Cheri speaks at women's conferences and events throughout the year and is a frequent guest on national radio and TV programs. Her articles on children, learning, and family life have been featured in *Focus on the Family, Family Circle, ParentLife, Guideposts,* and many other magazines. She's also a contributing editor for *Today's Christian Woman* and *PrayKids!* magazines. Her ministry Families Pray USA motivates and equips moms and dads, children, teens, and churches to impact their world through prayer. A former teacher, Cheri holds a Master's degree in English Literature and has wide experience teaching children, leading and speaking to mothers' groups, and raising her own kids.

She and her husband Holmes have three grown children, five grandchildren, and live in Oklahoma. Cheri's Internet site, www.cherifuller.com, includes her Mothering by Heart column for moms, resources and creative ideas on kids, building families, prayer, and more.

To contact Cheri for speaking engagements: Speak Up Speaker's Services, 810/982-0898 (phone); 810/987-4163 (fax); or *speakupinc@aol.com.*

FOCUS ON THE FAMILY®
Welcome to the Family!

Whether you received this book as a gift, borrowed it from
a friend, or purchased it yourself, we're glad you read it! It's just
one of the many helpful, insightful, and encouraging
resources produced by Focus on the Family.

In fact, that's what Focus on the Family is all about—providing inspiration, information, and biblically based advice to people in all stages of life.

It began in 1977 with the vision of one man, Dr. James Dobson, a licensed
psychologist and author of 16 best-selling books on marriage, parenting,
and family. Alarmed by the societal, political, and economic pressures
that were threatening the existence of the American family, Dr. Dobson
founded Focus on the Family with one employee—an assistant—
and a once-a-week radio broadcast, aired on only 36 stations.

Now an international organization, Focus on the Family is dedicated
to preserving Judeo-Christian values and strengthening the family
through more than 70 different ministries, including eight separate
daily radio broadcasts; television public service announcements;
10 publications; and a steady series of books and award-winning
films and videos for people of all ages and interests.

Recognizing the needs of, as well as the sacrifices and important
contributions made by, such diverse groups as educators, physicians,
attorneys, crisis pregnancy center staff, and single parents,
Focus on the Family offers specific outreaches to uphold and
minister to these individuals, too. And it's all done for one purpose,
and one purpose only: to encourage and strengthen individuals
and families through the life-changing message of Jesus Christ.

For more information about the ministry, or if we can be of help to your
family, simply write to Focus on the Family, Colorado Springs, CO 80995
or call 1-800-A-FAMILY (1-800-232-6459). Friends in Canada may write
Focus on the Family, P.O. Box 9800, Stn. Terminal, Vancouver, B.C. V6B 4G3.
or call 1-800-661-9800. Visit our Web site—www.family.org—to learn more about
the ministry or to find out if there is a Focus on the Family office in your country.

We'd love to hear from you!

Other Faith and Family Strengtheners
From Focus on the Family!®

Creative Correction

You may recognize her as the star of the hit '80s TV show "The Facts of Life." Now that she's the mother of three, Lisa Whelchel has some pertinent thoughts for parents who struggle with disciplining their children. *Creative Correction* draws from her own successes and mistakes to help other parents deal with sibling rivalry, lying and other behavioral challenges. Her creative, down-to-earth encouragement and biblical perspective provide a breath of fresh air to overwhelmed parents everywhere. Hardcover.

Parents' Guide to the Spiritual Growth of Children

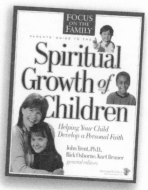

Building a foundation of faith in your children can be easy—and fun!—with help from the *Parents' Guide to the Spiritual Growth of Children*. Through simple and practical advice, this comprehensive guide shows you how to build a spiritual training plan for your family and explains what to teach your children at different ages. Hardcover.

Who Holds the Key to Your Heart?

In the hearts of most women lies a "secret place" containing hidden thoughts, painful experiences and emotions. Lysa TerKeurst, who has dealt with her own secret shame, will help you identify your pain and lead you to hope and healing through Scripture, testimonials, study questions and more. Come be renewed and break the bondage hidden in your secret place. Paperback.

Look for these special books in your Christian bookstore or request a copy by calling 1-800-A-FAMILY (1-800-232-6459). Friends in Canada may write to Focus on the Family, P.O. Box 9800, Stn. Terminal, Vancouver, B.C. V6B 4G3 or call 1-800-661-9800.